YELLOWSTONE FISHING GUIDE

3rd Edition

The Complete Guide To Fishing Yellowstone Waters

ROBERT CHARLTON

Photography by Dan Casali

Dedicated to Heather, Rebecca, Shawn and Cade,
that they may learn appreciation of the natural
wonders of this creation.

Acknowledgments

I would like to thank the many people who assisted me in putting this book together. Dan Carty, Fish and Wildlife Service biologist, critiqued the manuscript and provided expert suggestions. My publisher, Dan Casali, motivated me and reminded me of deadlines. My wife, Linda, tolerated my addiction to fishing. My children constantly interrupted me and reminded me of the true values of life. These people I thank wholeheartedly, along with many friends and fishing companions who cheerfully accompanied me on numerous fishing explorations, and still remained friends even when I led them to unproductive reaches.

Front cover design by Vickey Hanson
Maps by Dan Casali

ISBN 1-885719-00-0
Published by   Lost River Press
                 P.O. Box 1286
                 Ketchum, Idaho 83340
                 (208) 726-5120

Printed in Korea

TABLE OF CONTENTS

The lakes and streams in the Greater Yellowstone Area are found in some of the most beautiful settings in the world. The author hopes that you will enjoy your visit here as much as he enjoys this country. The book is written with reverence and appreciation for this land and it is hoped that every person who participates in these fisheries will make a sincere effort to protect and preserve them in every way possible.

GOOD FISHING!

INTRODUCTION

The ponds, lakes and streams of Yellowstone National Park offer some of the finest trout fishing in North America. Park visitors have the opportunity to catch good size wild cutthroat, rainbow, brown, and brook trout in a prime natural environment. Lake trout and whitefish are also available, and magnificent sail-finned grayling (extremely rare elsewhere in the lower forty-eight states) can be tempted by dainty dry flies.

The park includes over 400 fishable waters, including the huge (and hugely productive) Yellowstone River, the richly diverse Firehole, and the headwaters of the popular Madison—offering about 800 miles of flowing trout water in all. Of the hundreds of lakes in the park, many were once planted with trout. However, only a relative few provided suitable spawning grounds, or were able to sustain life through the bitter Rocky Mountain winter. Today there are forty-five fishable lakes in Yellowstone, including Shoshone Lake, the largest backcountry lake in the U.S. outside of Alaska, and Yellowstone Lake, whose enormous cutthroat trout average over fifteen inches in length. Over one half of the fish caught in the park are taken from Yellowstone Lake and Yellowstone River.

Recent angler surveys found that the typical park angler spends two days fishing in the park and usually fishes in more than one area each day. For every hour fished, about one fish was caught on the average. Over 90% of the fish caught were subsequently released. Of the fish reported landed, the majority were cutthroat trout, with rainbow, brook, and brown following in order. Small numbers of grayling, whitefish, lake trout, hybrid/cutthroat- rainbow, and nongame species were also landed. The current average size of fish landed in the park is approaching fourteen inches. Lake trout have

MADISON RIVER NEAR MADISON CAMPGROUND

the largest average size—over seventeen inches—and brook trout the smallest at under eight inches. Three pound trout are common, and five pounders raise few eyebrows.

The park also offers some of North America's most unique angling environments. Where else can you fish beside steaming geysers, or in the company of bison, bear, and moose? (Bear, moose, and bison have right-of-way on streamside.) Also, Yellowstone has few rivals to its annual wildflower display.

MANAGEMENT OF PARK FISHERIES

Yellowstone, America's first national park, was established in order to preserve its unique natural environment, and to provide an opportunity for future generations of visitors to see and appreciate native plant and animal life as it was found on the wild continent.

Fishing has always played a role in the life of the park, and it is now managed in a way that is consistent with the park's primary preservation goal. The Park Service views fishing by visitors as compatible with the purpose of Yellowstone National Park when it does not deny food that supports the fish-eating birds and animals, and does not impact native fish populations to the extent that their numbers decline.

Fish were first stocked in Yellowstone in the 1890s, and stocking continued up into the 1950s. This enthusiasm for stocking overlooked the impact of hatchery fish upon wild fish populations in the park, and by the '50s, scientific studies had demonstrated that the native fish of the park were being adversely affected by the stocking programs. Pure genetic strains of native cutthroat were becoming hybridized, and competition for food and shelter from hatchery trout was reducing native and wild trout populations. Stocking was discontinued.

Today, the fisheries management program within the park is administered by the U.S. Fish and Wildlife Service. Their published objectives are:

- To manage the fishery program as an integral part of the park ecosystem.
- To preserve and restore native species and aquatic habitats and
- To provide anglers with high-quality angling for wild fish in natural environments in a manner consistent with the first two objectives.

Regulations to restore or protect fisheries and maintain high quality angling have included manipulating season dates, restricting baits, establishing creel and size limits, and designating certain species or waters for catch and release fishing only. These management practices have improved fish populations, and fishing in Yellowstone today is superior to that found before the restrictions were implemented. Though not required by regulation to do so on all waters, anglers in Yellowstone are encouraged to preserve the fishing opportunities for future generations by releasing their fish.

FISHING THE MADISON RIVER

USING
THIS BOOK

Yellowstone Fishing Guide divides Yellowstone National Park into six zones (one per chapter), which are based upon the six primary watersheds within the park. Zone maps found at the beginning of each chapter locate all waters described in the succeeding text. The maps also depict major access trails and roads.

Within each chapter, water descriptions are arranged in alphabetical order. At the bottom of each left-hand page you will find, dictionary style, the name of the first water entry on the page; on the right-hand the name of the last water entry.

To speed location of entries on the zone map, each entry is accompanied by a miniature drawing of the zone divided into sections. The white section indicates where to look on the zone map to find the entry.

Within each write-up, access roads and trails are suggested. However, we advise you to refer to a current park map and consult a park ranger for specific directions from your starting point, and to determine current trail and road conditions.

This guide and its maps are not intended to replace topographic maps, which are useful references throughout the park, and essential for finding your way around Yellowstone's backcountry. Visitor centers in the park and local outdoor stores have hiking maps available for purchase.

Where first hand information was not available, I have included the results of the park's most recent angler surveys. In referring to this survey information, be advised that angler success is subject to variables such as time of year, location on the stream, and the reliability (and skill level) of the reporter. But I have found these reports useful in planning my own outings here, so offer them to you.

In reporting the results of angler survey data, the following scale is used:

Excellent: 80% and above of the respondents reporting satisfaction with experience, size and/or number of fish.

Above Average: 60 to 79% reporting satisfaction with experience, size and/or number of fish.

Average: 50 to 59% reporting satisfaction with experience, size and/or number of fish.

Below Average: Between 30 and 49% reporting satisfaction with experience, size and/or number of fish.

Poor: Below 29% of respondents reporting satisfaction with experience, size and/or number of fish.

Angler survey information is taken from Technical Reports compiled by the Fish and Wildlife Service, U.S. Department of the Interior, Yellowstone National Park.

LOWER GEYSER BASIN NEAR THE FIREHOLE RIVER

PLANNING YOUR TRIP

Yellowstone Lake and River receive the majority of the total park-wide angler use. The remaining usage is spread out over forty-five fishable lakes and 400 streams, with a mere thirty of them taking the bulk of the pressure. If you seek angling in solitude, you have many alternatives.

AVOIDING THE CROWDS

A short hike from the road is often all it takes to get away. Browse through the zone listings and the day hikes chapter in this book for possible destinations. Even popular waters like the Yellowstone River can be approached in relative seclusion by the angler willing to hike into the canyon—but pack your nitroglycerin capsules when you attempt this.

Contact a park ranger before you begin a day hike or overnight trip. Permits are required for some day hikes and all overnight trips. The park has a designated backcountry campsite reservation system and a non-fee permit and reserved campsite is required for an overnight stay. Permits can only be obtained in person and no more than 48 hours in advance. Pets are prohibited in the backcountry.

A boat can take you into the back country on several lakes. Be sure to obtain a boating permit (available for a fee at any ranger station) prior to setting out. Heed the advice provided with the permit—the cold waters of Yellowstone's lakes have claimed many victims. A Coast Guard approved flotation device is required for each person on board.

You may escape much of the crowd by planning your trip for September, after Labor Day. The weather is often quite pleasant, but even more capricious than in summer. Plan for a bit of rain or snow.

If its really crowded and you aren't up to hiking, consider trying some of the excellent waters in the area surrounding the park. See the chapter on the fishing available in the Greater Yellowstone Area.

CONSIDER THE CLIMATE

Those who are unfamiliar with Yellowstone should keep in mind that this is high altitude terrain, with most elevations in the park standing 7000 feet or greater above sea level. Days are pleasantly cool, and nights are chilly. The temperature can be expected to drop below freezing any month of the year at night. Daytime temperatures typically reach 75°F during the warmest month, August.

The season for the angler at Yellowstone runs roughly from ice-out in late May through the snows of October. Early season fishing is

STORM MOVING OVER FIREHOLE RIVER

pretty much restricted to lakes, as winter runoff muddies the streams well into July most years. Fishing can be very good in late July.

Mosquitoes are an unwelcome early season bonus, peaking with the wildflowers through July and into early August. By late August they cease to be a problem. Backcountry explorers often prefer the month of August for its milder nights, bug-free days, and good fishing.

By late September, hillsides shimmer golden-yellow as aspen tremble in the wind. Waters run low and clear, and the stream angler must be prepared to stalk his prey. This is the favorite time for many park regulars. The summer crowds have thinned, and the crisp air crackles with the rapidly advancing fall. A few snows can be expected. By October you can expect sub-zero night temperatures and the first of the heavy snows.

Weather at Yellowstone is notoriously unpredictable and can change rapidly. Snowfalls can occur during any month of the year. A day which begins sunny and mild can develop within a few hours into showers or even mountain shaking, hail spitting thunderstorms.

Even on a mid-summer day hike it's prudent to pack along extra clothing, such as a warm sweater, extra wool socks, and a lightweight rainproof jacket. It tends to rain a lot in Yellowstone. And don't forget the bug juice.

EFFECTS OF THE 1988 YELLOWSTONE FIRES

America held its breath as the fires of Yellowstone raged in the summer of 1988. Those who had visited the park, or who meant to someday, worried about survival of the park's scenic treasures and abundant wildlife... and wondered what would be left.

Today one cannot avoid seeing blackened stands of lodgepole pine throughout much of the park, but the forest floor is brilliant green with the vigorous resurgence of new growth. Fire has long been a presence in these lands, and the vegetation has long adapted to it. It is also much easier now to spot big game animals within these thinned forest stands.

SNAGS ON MADISON RIVER

The burned areas of the park have been well surveyed and mapped. Approximately one third of the park was affected by the fires. However, only about half of the affected acreage experienced canopy burn, where needles or leaves and many smaller branches were consumed and trees totally blackened and died.

Fishery biologists have completed extensive studies of many streams impacted by extensive burn areas. Their findings suggest that the negative fire effects on fish populations were minimal and of short duration.

Still-standing fire killed trees, or snags, can present a danger to the park visitor unfortunate enough to be present when they finally fall. Avoiding areas with large numbers of dead trees is prudent, especially during windstorms. Even on relatively calm days, these snags can fall without warning. Be cautious.

WILD COUNTRY PRECAUTIONS

Few people among the millions of Yellowstone visitors have been injured by wildlife, and the majority of them were reaping the harvest

KEEP YOUR FOOD AWAY FROM BEARS

of extremely poor judgment. Bear, moose, elk, and bison are powerful, untamed creatures well deserving of your respect. A modicum of prudence will make it most unlikely that you will have a close encounter of the worst kind. Don't try to feed the animals, don't get between a mom and her kids, and keep a respectful distance. Don't keep food in your tent. Common sense stuff. The park service will provide you with pamphlets full of helpful suggestions. Use your head.

Yellowstone is bear country, and noisy hikers are least likely to surprise bears. Loud and continuous talking, wearing a bell, or letting a can of rattling pebbles dangle from your pack as you walk may save you from an unpleasant surprise.

FISHING GEAR RECOMMENDATIONS

There are excellent tackle shops near each park entrance, staffed by personnel who will gladly provide seasoned advice. You really should plan to spend some time in one of the local shops for an up-to-the-minute briefing and best tips on tackle and location.

For stream fishing, a small-meshed landing net and a pair of chest waders are recommended. Chest waders offer more versatility than hip boots, allowing you to access the most consistently good sections of both lakes and streams, and providing insulation against cold water temperatures. Waders are not made for walking long distances, so bring good hiking shoes for the trail.

In general, leaders from two to four pounds are usually sufficient for stream fishing, while heavier gear is required for trolling lakes. If you are dry fly fishing, you will find that very small flies and

THE BASIC SPINNING OUTFIT

- Medium weight ($6\frac{1}{2}$ or 7 foot) rod with six pound test line on an open or closed face spinning reel.
- Several plastic bubbles for casting flies.
- Number 4, 6, and 9 Panther Martin spinners in yellow, black, or red colors.
- Number 2 Mepps spinners in gold and silver (gold seems to do better with cutthroat, silver with rainbow).
- Daredevils and Spoons in the smaller sizes ($\frac{1}{4}$ to $\frac{1}{2}$ ounce). Red and white, bright orange, copper and brass are favorite colors, especially on Yellowstone Lake.
- Jake's Spin A Lure ($\frac{1}{4}$ ounce) gold and silver.
- Assorted wet flies, nymphs and some basic dry fly patterns.
- Fjord Spoons (heavier weights for lakes).

light leaders are necessary later in the season, especially among the wary (and well educated) trout of the park's most accessible waters. Remember that the use of barbless hooks allows the angler to release fish much easier and limits tissue damage.

Spin Fishing

On smaller streams, the spinner type lures that do not sink as rapidly seem to do better. At times, a bubble and fly combination is excellent on the lakes and should not be overlooked, especially if you see surface activity and do not have a fly rod.

If you are new to the park and want to troll, ask the guides at the marinas for suggestions. Their advice on where to start and how deep to fish will save you a lot of time. For deep trolling on the lakes, use leaded lines that are color coded so you can keep track of the depth you fish. Lead core trolling lines are not included in the new lead-free restrictions.

When fishing from the shoreline on those lakes that are closed to motorized water craft, try the following technique. First, locate some likely looking structure (rocky point, drop off, inlet, etc.) and wade out as deep as your waders permit. Use one of your heavier lures (Fjord Spoons work well), and cast it as far as you can. Count until your lure reaches the bottom, then reel it in. On the next cast, allow the lure to sink, but begin retrieving a few numbers before your lure reaches the bottom. With this method, you will be fishing close to the bottom and can cover the depths efficiently. This method has proved especially effective for taking lake trout and the big cutthroat of Heart Lake.

A good technique to try when fishing the streams is to cast a small spinner upstream, reeling it in just a bit faster than the current.

FLY ANGLERS ON THE UPPER FIREHOLE RIVER

THE BASIC FLY OUTFIT

An 8½ foot fly rod for a 6 or 7weight line, with both floating double taper and sinking weight forward lines.

DRY FLIES — Sizes #12 through #18:

Adams	Ginger Quill	Gray Hackle Yellow
Light Cahill	Olive Dun light	Olive Dun dark
Renegade	Royal Wulff	Poly-wing spinners
Sofa Pillow	H & L Variant	Green Drake
Humpy	Quill Gordon	Blue Dun
Elk-hair Caddis	Kings River Caddis	

A good grasshopper imitation (Dave's or Whit's Hopper)

WET FLIES AND NYMPHS — Sizes #4 to #12:

Muddler Minnow	Zug Bug	Yellow Grey Hackle
Montana Nymph	Otter Nymph	Renegade
Black Nymph	Bitch Creek	Mormon Girl
Ginger Quill	Woolly Bugger	Leadwing Coachman
Midge Pupae	Caddis Pupae	Black Woollyworm
Olive Woollyworm	Gold Ribbed Hare's Ear	

FLY FISHING

Bring leaders varying between 1 1/2 pound to three pounds and good fly dope to keep the dry flies on top of the water. A float tube and neoprene waders make a dandy outfit for exploring the fishable lakes. Remember that float tubes are not allowed on streams, with the exception of the Lewis River Channel. Float tubes are classified as boats and therefore require the user to purchase a non-motorized boat permit.

Fly patterns can be obtained at most of the local tackle shops at the entrances to the park and also within the park at several of the

MAJOR YELLOWSTONE HATCHES

May Flies (Early Season)

Light Olive Duns

Firehole	June 10 to July 15
Madison	June 15 to July 15

Green Drakes

Madison	June 15 to July 15

May Flies (Mid-Season)

General

Yellowstone R.	July 15 to September 30
Madison	August 25 to October 30
Firehole	September 1 to October 30

Gray Drake

Yellowstone R.	July 20 to August 1

Light Olive Duns

Slough Creek	July 25 to September 1

May Flies (Late Season)

Blue Winged Olive

Madison	September 1 to October 15
Firehole	September 15 to October 30

Caddis Flies

All streams	June through August

Dragon Flies

Firehole	June 10 to August 15

Stone Flies

Gallatin	July 10 to July 25
Yellowstone R.	July 10 to August 1

Terrestrials

Hoppers, Ants, Beetles

Madison	July 15 to September 15
Gallatin	August 1 to September 1
Firehole	August 1 to September 15
Gardner	August 1 to September 15
Yellowstone R.	August 1 to September 15

Pine Moth

Gallatin	July 25 to August 15

Hatch information provided courtesy The Trout Shop, West Yellowstone, Montana

FISHING COMPANIONS ON THE MADISON RIVER

larger stores. Be sure to ask about the hatches currently taking place or about to occur. Anglers are encouraged to discontinue the use of flies weighted by lead wire although the complete ban on lead weighted flies won't be in effect until later.

If you are in the park around July 15, the stonefly hatch will be proceeding up the Hayden Valley toward Yellowstone Lake. Terrific fly fishing with stonefly imitations begins around that time.

CHECK PARK REGULATIONS CAREFULLY BEFORE KEEPING A FISH

FISHING REGULATIONS

Fishing regulations are frequently revised to respond to changing conditions. Regulations may vary greatly from area to area within the park. *Be certain to get a copy of the most recent regulations upon entering the park.*

All anglers twelve years of age and older are required to obtain a fishing permit prior to fishing park waters. Fishing in Yellowstone is no longer free. Starting with the 1994 season, anglers 16 years of age and older must pay for the privilege of fishing Yellowstone's famous waters. These adult anglers may purchase as seven day permit for $5.00 or a season permit for $10.00. Anglers between 12 and 15 years must obtain a free permit, while those under 12 may fish without a permit. Permits may be obtained at ranger stations and visitor centers throughout the park, as well as at some sporting goods stores in the areas surrounding the park. You may also obtain a permit by mail by writing the Visitor Services Office, P.O. Box 168, Yellowstone National Park, WY 82190.

All of the money generated from the sale of permits will remain in the park to support Yellowstone fisheries. Permits are sold in the park and in many of the sporting good stores surrounding the park. The fee for fishing is minimal and certainly well spent in funding a first-rate fishing program.

Maps and regulations are free and may be obtained at the entrance gates. Ranger stations have the necessary permits and area maps. The park rangers are there to assist you, and you should feel free to turn to them for information concerning park regulations or current fishing, boating, and hiking conditions.

The fishing season in Yellowstone is from the first Saturday of Memorial Day weekend through the first Sunday in November. A major exception is Yellowstone Lake, which opens on June 15th. *Other exceptions exist; check current regulations.*

Bait angling is, in general, prohibited in the park. A special exception exists for children 11 years or younger; they may use worms as bait on the Gardner River, and Indian, Obsidian and Panther Creeks *only.*

Yellowstone National Park recently implemented a lead-free fishing program. Lead products such as lead sinkers, lead-headed jigs and lead wrap-ons are no longer allowed to be used in the Park. Anglers are encouraged to discontinue the use of flies weighted by lead wire although the complete ban on lead weighted flies won't be in effect until later. Lead core trolling lines are not included in the current restrictions.

Yellowstone National Park fisheries are managed according to species rather than on a water by water basis. *At this writing,* the following species restrictions are in effect:

Cutthroat Trout are restricted to catch and release fishing throughout the park, except in Yellowstone Lake, in the Lamar River and its tributaries upstream from Calfee Creek, and in the Soda Butte Creek Drainage. Be sure to check current regulations for catch and size limits applying to these waters.

Grayling are restricted to catch-and-release throughout the park with no exceptions.

Rainbow Trout are restricted to catch and release throughout the park except for the Soda Butte Creek drainage and its tributaries, where currently two fish over 13 inches may be kept.

Brown Trout are available to keep at a rate of two fish per day, any size, except in the Madison, Firehole, and the Gibbon River below Gibbon Falls, where keepers must be under 10 inches. Fishing for browns is restricted to catch and release only in the Lewis River below Lewis Falls to Lewis Canyon.

Mountain Whitefish may be kept at a rate of two fish per day, any size.

Brook Trout have a Park-wide regulation of five fish per day which must be under 10 inches in length.

Lake Trout are available to keep at a rate of two fish per day any size.

GAMEFISH IDENTIFICATION

Many species of fish inhabit the park waters. Since park fisheries are managed by species, you must learn to distinguish one fish species from another or run the danger of an embarrassing (and expensive) regulation violation. Following is a brief description of the primary game fish within the park. For a more comprehensive review of the fish species inhabiting Yellowstone Park, visit the Yellowstone Aquatic Library in Mammoth.

Cutthroat Trout Red slashes in the throat region give this trout its name. It is the most frequently landed fish in the park and provides novice anglers the greatest opportunity for success. Research suggests that the cutthroat is twice as catchable as the brook trout and almost twelve times as catchable as the brown.

To counter their gullibility, cutthroat are protected by more regulations than other species in the park, though they do have other natural advantages working in their favor as well. As one of the area's native species, cutthroat are adaptable to a greater variety of environments, and being less territorial than their cousins, can live comfortably in

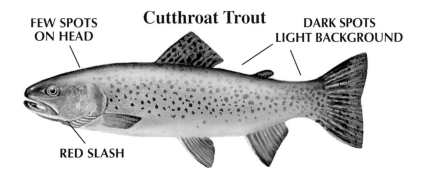

FEW SPOTS
ON HEAD

Cutthroat Trout

DARK SPOTS
LIGHT BACKGROUND

RED SLASH

greater population densities. There is some evidence that where native cutthroat were displaced by other trout species, the newcomers did not achieve the average or maximum sizes of the natives. Maximum life expectancy for cutthroat approaches ten years, with the trout reaching maturity at about four years.

Grayling Grayling are distinguished by a small mouth and a large, brilliantly iridescent dorsal fin. Their range within the park is limited, with the most consistent catches in Cascade, Grebe and Wolf Lakes. Occasional catches (rare) are reported from the Gibbon and Madison Rivers, and there was one unsuccessful attempt to reintroduce them into Canyon Creek.

Grayling are easy to take on flies. They live about seven years, maturing at age three, and reach a length of about eleven inches. The killing or possession of grayling is prohibited, and all must be returned unharmed to the water.

Grayling

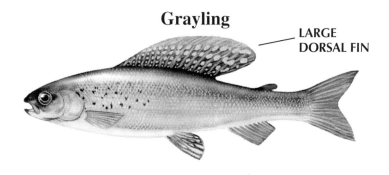

LARGE
DORSAL FIN

Brown Trout This trout is usually identified by the many red or orange spots on its side. It may also have an orange or yellow margin on its fins. Wary and easily disturbed, brown trout are difficult to catch, frustrating to inexperienced anglers, and do not require the protective regulations of other species. They usually mature in three years at a length of about eleven inches. Old Browns grow very large indeed. Brown trout are highly territorial, with the larger fish

Brown Trout

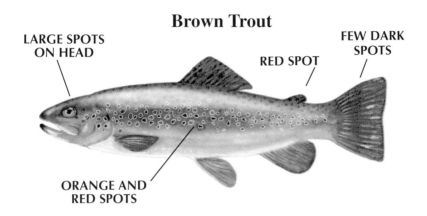

LARGE SPOTS
ON HEAD

FEW DARK
SPOTS

RED SPOT

ORANGE AND
RED SPOTS

winning the best locations. They have a reputation for feeding at night, mainly on other fish. An European species, Browns were first introduced into park waters in 1890. Less tolerant of warm water than cutthroat or rainbow, they move into the upper reaches of the rivers to spawn in October, November, and December.

Rainbow Trout   The pink or red band on its sides gives this species its distinguishing characteristic. Rainbow trout are native to the northern Pacific coast, and were introduced into park waters during the 1920's. They have a reputation for fast growth and impressive acrobatics when hooked. Like the cutthroat, rainbow trout are very adaptable, able to live and thrive in waters other trout cannot tolerate. In the geothermally heated Firehole River, rainbow seem

Rainbow Trout

NUMEROUS SPOTS
ON HEAD

DARK SPOTS, LIGHT
BACKGROUND

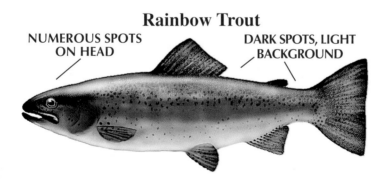

comfortable in water temperatures approaching 80° F. Rainbow mature at age two years when they average ten inches in length. Rainbow and cutthroats often produce a hybrid strain in waters they cohabit.

Brook Trout This trout is identified by worm-like markings on its back, and by red, pink or yellow dots and often a bluish halo covering its sides. It has dark and light bands on its fins, and a reddish-orange fringe on its underside. Brook trout have a tendency to overpopulate, which leads to a small average size in many waters.

Brook Trout

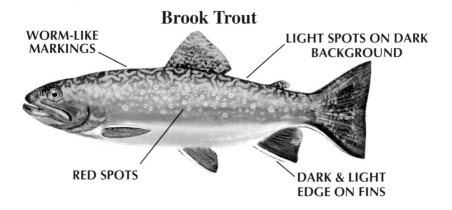

WORM-LIKE MARKINGS

LIGHT SPOTS ON DARK BACKGROUND

RED SPOTS

DARK & LIGHT EDGE ON FINS

They mature fast and have a short life span. Vulnerable to angling pressure, they are easily caught by inexperienced anglers. Yet another introduced species, Brook trout are native to eastern North America.

Lake Trout Lake trout are distinguished by their deeply forked tail, pointed head and jaw, and a back covered with large whitish spots on a dark background. They grow slowly, have a long life span, and are the largest fish in Yellowstone, reaching fifteen to twenty inches in length at maturity, and living five to fifteen years. They eat mostly fish. In recent years anglers have reported catches of lake trout weighing between ten and twenty pounds. Lake trout are not native to Yellowstone, having been planted in the historically fishless Lewis

Lake Trout

**WORM-LIKE
MARKINGS**

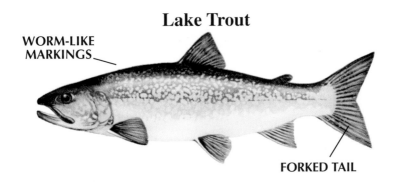

FORKED TAIL

and Shoshone Lakes. They are also found in Heart Lake and its drainage. Lake trout are rarely caught on flies except just after ice-out, when they cruise the shallows for a few weeks.

Mountain Whitefish The whitefish has a round or oblong body and a small, toothless mouth with an overhanging snout. It has a light silvery color on the sides and white on the belly. A Yellowstone native, whitefish are very sensitive to their environment, which restricts their range and distribution. With a growth rate slower than that of trout, whitefish reach only eight to ten inches at maturity. They have shown an ability to withstand heavy fishing pressure, proving more difficult to catch than many of the park's trout species. A popular belief that mountain whitefish compete with trout for food has not been demonstrated in recent studies. The whitefish has the strength and weight to provide a satisfying fishing experience.

Mountain Whitefish

**SMALL MOUTH
NO TEETH**

THE GRAND CANYON OF THE YELLOWSTONE - UPPER FALLS

ZONE 1

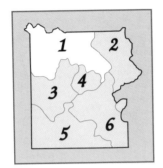

Including the Gallatin and Gardner River watersheds, and the Yellowstone River watershed from the north boundary upstream to Inspiration Point, excluding the Lamar River.

The rugged peaks, steep ridges, and narrow valleys of this area hold the small streams and lakes that source the Gallatin and Gardner Rivers. This zone also features the Yellowstone River drainage from Canyon Village to the north boundary, including the river's Black Canyon and the Grand Canyon of the Yellowstone. Beyond the canyons, the Yellowstone flows through relatively flat terrain. Because it is at a lower elevation, spring, summer, and good fishing arrive earlier in this section than elsewhere in the park.

Wildlife is abundant throughout this zone. There are frequent sightings of deer, elk, bighorn sheep, and some moose. Grizzly bear activity often closes the trails, so check with a park ranger for current conditions before starting out.

Major access to this part of the park is via Highway 191 north from West Yellowstone, and the West Entrance Road to the Grand Loop Road (Norris to Mammoth to Tower Falls).

This section of the park is popular with families, since children eleven years and younger may fish with worms as bait in the Gardner River and in Obsidian, Indian, and Panther creeks. These are the only waters in the park that may be fished with natural bait.

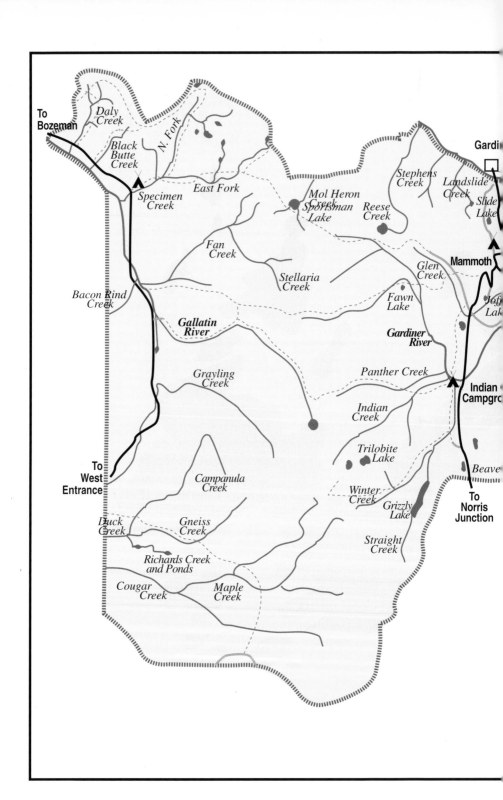

ZONE 1

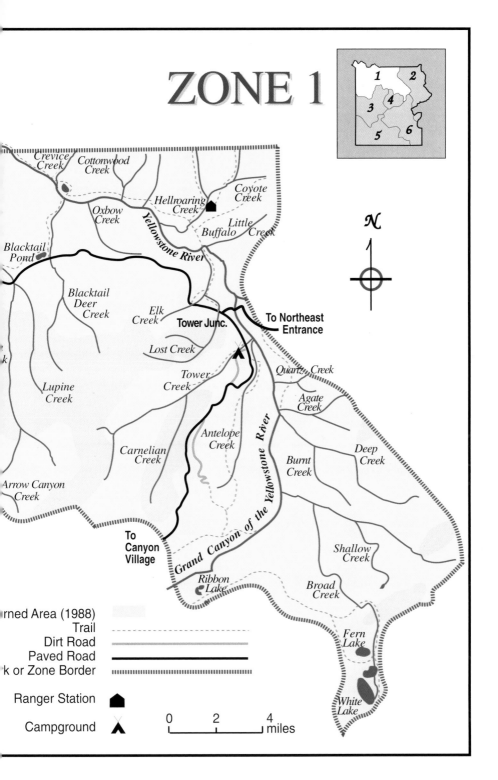

Crevice Creek
Cottonwood Creek
Coyote Creek
Oxbow Creek
Hellroaring Creek
Little Buffalo Creek
Yellowstone River
Blacktail Pond
Blacktail Deer Creek
Elk Creek
Tower Junc.
To Northeast Entrance
Lost Creek
Quartz Creek
Lupine Creek
Tower Creek
Agate Creek
Antelope Creek
Deep Creek
Carnelian Creek
Burnt Creek
Arrow Canyon Creek
Grand Canyon of the Yellowstone River
To Canyon Village
Shallow Creek
Ribbon Lake
Broad Creek
Fern Lake
White Lake

ᴺ

Burned Area (1988)
Trail
Dirt Road
Paved Road
Park or Zone Border

Ranger Station
Campground

0   2   4 miles

Accommodations are available outside the park at West Yellowstone and Gardiner, and inside the park at Mammoth Hot Springs. There are campgrunds at Norris, Indian Creek, and Mammoth, and Forest Service campgrounds outside the Park in the Gardner and West Yellowstone areas.

Agate Creek

One of several creeks draining into the Yellowstone River from the east, accessed by the Specimen Ridge Trail. It contains small trout near its confluence with the Yellowstone.

There is a trail leading down to the confluence from the Specimen Ridge Trail. The Specimen Ridge trailhead is on the Northeast Entrance Road, about a mile from Tower Junction. The spur trail down to the Yellowstone is about four miles long. Anglers also use this spur to fish Burnt and Deep creeks, but it is primarily an access to the Yellowstone. The creek's upper waters are apparently fishless.

Antelope Creek

A low-rated brook trout stream, followed by the Grand Loop Road for several miles south of Tower Falls. It contains a few pan-size brook trout averaging over seven inches with a catch rate that exceeds one fish per hour.

Arrow Canyon Creek

Tributary of Lava Creek, containing small brook trout. To reach it, follow Lava Creek upstream from the crossing of the Grand Loop Road east of Mammoth.

Bacon Rind Creek

A small creek crossed by Highway 191 about 24 miles north of West Yellowstone. It contains cutthroat and rainbow trout. The fish average nine inches, and landing rates exceed one fish per hour. Angler satisfaction is above average for experience, numbers of fish caught, and for size.

Beaver Lake

A brook trout lake just west of the Grand Loop Road, about five miles north of Norris Junction. It contains a population of brook trout, although little is known of angler success. There is a picnic area near the lake.

Black Butte Creek

A small tributary of the Gallatin, near Daly Creek. Recent stream surveys suggest it does not support a population of resident catchable trout.

Blacktail Deer Creek

A good brook trout stream, tributary of the Yellowstone. It is crossed by the Grand Loop Road approximately one mile east of the road's Lava Creek crossing. The Blacktail Trailhead begins near the bridge, following the creek downstream to its confluence, a descent of a thousand feet to a beautiful stretch of the Black Canyon.

To fish upstream, just follow the creek. It offers good fishing for brook trout to ten inches. Recent landing rates exceed two fish per hour. Anglers report above average satisfaction with numbers caught and over-all experience, but only average satisfaction with size of fish.

Blacktail Pond

A popular and very accessible brook and cutthroat trout pond near Mammoth. Traveling east on the Grand Loop Road towards Tower Junction, you will see Blacktail on your left, about seven miles out of Mammoth. There is a parking turn-out with an easy trail down to the water.

The pond is about eleven acres with maximum depth about twenty-six feet. Primarily spring fed, it offers little natural spawning ground for the less adaptable cutthroat. The small cutthroat population here is protected by catch-and-release restrictions.

BLACKTAIL POND

Brook trout seem to be thriving, however. The average catch here approaches fourteen inches. Landing rate is nearly one fish per hour, with an above average number of anglers satisfied with all aspects of their experience. The terrain around Blacktail can be marshy, so you might want to wear boots or waders.

Broad Creek

A substantial cutthroat trout creek that flows out of the Fern Lake/White Lake basin beneath Stonetop Mountain. It enters the Grand Canyon of the Yellowstone from the east.

You can reach the upper stretch of Broad Creek by following the Wapiti Lake Trail. The trail can be taken from the Upper Falls or Artist Point across the river from Canyon Village. Broad Creek supports a population of cutthroat trout which average twelve inches. Landing rates over one fish per hour are reported, with excellent satisfaction with the experience and the size and numbers of fish caught. The Wapiti Lake Trail is frequently used as a means to access the off-trail geothermal sites of the Mirror Plateau.

Burnt Creek

A tributary of Deep Creek, accessed by way of the Specimen Ridge Trail. It joins Deep Creek just before its confluence with the Yellowstone. To reach both creeks, take the Specimen Ridge Trail into the canyon to the junction of the Agate Creek spur trail, following the spur about four miles to Agate's confluence with the Yellowstone. Then proceed upstream along the Yellowstone less than a mile to Deep Creek. Following Deep Creek upstream, you will find Burnt Creek pouring in from the right. Like Deep and Agate, Burnt Creek has a population of small trout in its lowest reach.

Campanula Creek (See Duck Creek.)

Carnelian Creek

A tributary of Tower Creek, flowing north off Dunraven Peak. It joins Tower about four miles south-west of Tower Falls Campground. A trail heading southwest from the camp reaches Carnelian at about mile four. Both Tower and Carnelian contain rainbow and brook trout. The trout average eight inches in length with landing rates of over four fish per hour being reported. Excellent satisfaction ratings are usual for this fishery.

Cottonwood Creek

Tributary of the Yellowstone near the north boundary, offering excellent fishing for cutthroat averaging thirteen inches in length. It enters the Yellowstone east of the Blacktail Trail Bridge. Turn right onto the Yellowstone Trail after crossing the river. Cottonwood Creek is the second stream you will come to. Anglers rate their experience on Cottonwood as excellent, with a landing rate of over two fish per hour.

Cougar Creek

Cougar and nearby Maple Creeks can be reached by following the directions to Duck Creek, but instead of following the road to the left at the park boundary, follow the car tracks to the right which lead to Maple Creek.

Cougar used to be joined by Maple Creek just upstream from the highway crossing. Currently it appears to disappear into a meadow. To reach it, follow Maple Creek upstream.

The Gneiss Creek Trail crosses an upper stretch of Cougar Creek. Gneiss Creek Trail, heads north from the West Entrance Road between West Yellowstone and Madison Junction, about seven miles from the West Entrance.

Satisfaction with the fishing on Cougar Creek varies greatly from year to year, with anglers in recent years giving this creek ratings that vary from excellent to poor for total experience and numbers of fish caught. Landing rates are generally more than two fish per hour, with a catch averaging seven inches.

Coyote Creek

A tributary of Hellroaring Creek offering good fishing for eleven-inch cutthroat. It can be reached by the Coyote Creek Trail or the Hellroaring Trail. Both trails lead into the Absaroka Primitive Area of the Gallatin National Forest. A Montana state license is required to fish Coyote beyond the park boundary. The prominent cone to the west is Hellroaring Mountain, one of the few granite peaks in the park.

Crevice Creek

Tributary of the Yellowstone above Knowles Falls, providing fair fishing for pan-size trout, probably cutthroat. To reach it, follow the Blacktail Trail to its junction with the Yellowstone River Trail. Bear left at the junction, keeping an eye out for the trail sign for Crevice Creek and the ranger station.

Daly Creek

A small mountain stream in the lightly visited northwest corner of the park. It joins the Gallatin River after meandering through a pretty valley dotted with aspen groves and offering handsome mountain vistas.

Daly contains cutthroat trout averaging ten inches and can be reached by way of the Daly Creek Trail, which heads at the confluence of Daly Creek and the Gallatin River along Highway 191, thirty miles north of West Yellowstone. Landing rates that exceed two fish per hour are reported.

Deep Creek

Joins the Yellowstone from the east in the lower Grand Canyon area. Small trout can be found near the creek's confluence with the Yellowstone. Otherwise, the creek is fishless. To access the confluence, follow the Specimen Ridge Trail east from the Northeast Entrance Road. Take the spur trail that leads down to the river (at the mouth of Agate Creek, a four mile hike), then proceed upstream along the Yellowstone less than a mile.

Duck Creek

A fine, meandering meadow stream with some deep holes holding good size trout that average fifteen inches. Duck Creek and its tributaries contain brown, brook and rainbow trout. At times fishing here has been rated excellent.

To reach the creek, follow Highway 191 north eight miles from West Yellowstone. Watch for a sign on the right. Turn right at the sign and keep right one mile until you reach the telephone line that marks the park boundary. The road to the left leads to a parking area and the head of Gneiss Creek Trail. The trail follows the north bank of Duck, skirting most of the marshy areas. Plan to get wet if you aren't wearing rubber boots.

Campanula, Gneiss, and Richards creeks join to form Duck about one mile upstream from the head of Gneiss Creek Trail. At the confluence, Campanula Creek is to the left and Richards Creek is to the right. The main trail follows Gneiss Creek, crossing it and continuing on into the beautiful Madison Valley. There is often a designated camp at Gneiss Creek.

There are some small springs emptying into Duck Creek, so be careful to remain on the forks containing the most water. Gneiss Creek joins from the east, and the three tributaries form a semicircle with Duck Creek receiving the water. Richards Creek is the better tributary to fish, although during spawning season the others will hold large fish.

Fly anglers should come prepared with small dry flies (especially caddis), and dragonfly and damselfly nymphs. Be sure to bring grasshopper imitations in late July and August.

Angler satisfaction with Duck Creek is often reported as excellent in all rating categories (experience, size, and numbers of fish caught)with landing rates that approach one fish per hour.

Elk Creek

A good brook trout stream, crossed by the Grand Loop Road west of Tower Junction. It is joined by its larger tributary, Lost Creek, about two miles downstream of the Garnet Hill trailhead. The Garnet Hill Trail then parallels Elk to its confluence with the Yellowstone. Brook trout averaging eight inches are found in both Elk and Lost, with larger fish available in the lower section near the Yellowstone. Landing rates of over two fish per hour are usual.

Fan Creek

A small spring-fed creek with a good reputation. It enters the Gallatin close to Highway 191, approximately twenty-two miles from West Yellowstone. It contains cutthroat and rainbow trout averaging nine inches.

The Fawn Pass Trail crosses Fan Creek and follows it a short distance, providing some access. Angler

TRUMPETER SWANS

surveys have reported excellent ratings both for size of the fish and numbers caught. Landing rates of less than one fish per hour have been reported.

Fawn Lake

 A marshy lake in the North Gardners Hole area, south of the Fawn Pass Trail about three miles west of the trail's intersection with the Glen Creek Service Road. The lake is visible a short distance south of the trail.

It supports a population of brook trout averaging twelve inches, with reported landing rates approaching two fish per hour. Anglers report excellent satisfaction with their experience here, with size of fish, and with numbers caught. Marshy terrain makes fishing portions of the lake difficult, and aquatic plant growth makes fishing from shore almost impossible in late summer.

Fern Lake

 A cutthroat lake north of Pelican Valley, above the northern end of Yellowstone Lake. It is reached by following the Pelican Creek Trail to the Astringent Creek Trail, which continues north to Fern. The approximate distance is eleven miles one way, beginning at the Pelican trailhead at the end of the service road about three miles from Fishing Bridge on the East Entrance Road. The lake covers about ninety acres, with maximum depth twenty-five feet. It is set in a heavily wooded area, with hot springs near the east shore. A return trip by way of the Pelican Creek Trail (about sixteen miles), leads past some interesting geothermal features, including The Mudkettles and The Mushpots. Other fishable waters in the area include Pelican Creek, Broad Creek, and White Lake.

Fern Lake supports a small population of cutthroat trout that apparently immigrated into the lake from Broad Creek. Fishing is reported as marginal.

Gallatin River

Headwaters of one of Montana's major fisheries. Though the most famous portion of the river is outside park boundaries, the headwaters offer good fishing, especially in the back-country stretch.

The river forms as the outlet of Gallatin Lake, below Three Rivers Peak. The Big Horn Pass Trail provides access to the upper stream, which meanders through a big meadowland.

The meadow portion of the river is easy to fish and easy to wade, with undercut banks, plenty of good holes, and unlimited backcasting room. To reach the trail, follow Highway 191 north from West Yellowstone about twenty-two miles to a spur road that leads east about a mile past Divide Lake.

Within the park, the Gallatin contains primarily cutthroat, rainbow, and whitefish averaging thirteen inches. Fishing success has been variable, with the best catches reported in the more inaccessible areas. Most anglers, however, fish along the roadside, reporting catches of under one fish per hour.

Anglers rate this river above average in size of fish and over-all angling experience, and below average for numbers caught.

Gardner River

A good tributary of the Yellowstone River, formed in the high country below Electric Peak near the north boundary, and joining the Yellowstone at Gardiner.

The Gardner offers good fishing for small, plentiful brook trout above Osprey Falls, where there are special regulations that allow children eleven or under to use worms as bait. Below the falls, which head the spectacular Sheepeater Canyon, the river attracts more serious anglers, challenged by its pocket water and larger fish.

Sportsman Lake Trail and Fawn Pass Trail both cross the upper backcountry waters. Howard Eaton Trail provides easy access from Indian Creek Campground north into the Gardners Hole area. The lower river is closely followed by the Grand Loop Road and the North Entrance Road.

The lower river contains brook, brown, rainbow, and some cutthroat trout. Nymph fishing can be effective here throughout the season. Grasshopper imitations work well in late summer. Browns from the Yellowstone River enter the Gardner on their spawning run in fall.

Anglers land fewer than two fish per hour, assigning an excellent rating for over-all experience, and above average satisfaction with the number and sizes landed. Eighty percent of the fishing pressure occurs below Osprey Falls.

Glen Creek

 A small tributary of the Gardner River with easy access from the Grand Loop Road and the Sportsman Lake Trail. It offers fair fishing for pan-size brook trout. Anglers rate their experience on the creek above average, but indicate dissatisfaction with the numbers and sizes of fish caught.

Gneiss Creek (See Duck Creek.)

Grayling Creek

 A spring-fed stream that flows into Hebgen Lake near West Yellowstone. Highway 191 parallels the creek for several miles, beginning about eight miles north of town. Whitefish, rainbow, cutthroat, and brown trout can be taken here, and there is a late fall spawning run of big browns from Hebgen Lake.

Upstream a few miles beyond the highway where the terrain flattens out, the creek has carved deeper holes where larger resident trout may be found. For about three miles above Grayling Falls the stream sees little angling pressure and can be pretty good. Smaller fish are characteristic of the upper waters, with the highest reaches too shallow to support many trout.

Grayling is difficult to fish due to willows and boggy conditions. Landing rates of over one fish per hour are reported. Over-all experience ratings are above average, as are the ratings for numbers and size of fish caught. The trout average over eight inches in length.

GARDNER RIVER

GRAYLING CREEK

Grizzly Lake

A long, beautiful lake nestled between two ridges, offering excellent fishing for brook trout that average eight inches.

It is reached by a strenuous two mile hike on the Grizzly Lake Trail, which heads west off the Grand Loop Road about eight miles north of Norris Junction. A landing rate of almost two fish per hour has been reported, with excellent ratings for over-all experience and numbers caught, and above average rating for size of fish. The lake is fed and drained by Straight Creek.

Hellroaring Creek

A cutthroat stream, tributary of the Yellowstone in the Black Canyon stretch, entering the river from the north. The Garnet Hill Trail at Tower Junction will take you to a footbridge across the Yellowstone.

If you can withstand the temptation to fish the Yellowstone, continue on the trail until you reach the Hellroaring Creek Trail. You can fish downstream or upstream from this point. The trail parallels the creek upstream, so access is no problem. There is a footbridge across the creek at the trail junction and another one-half mile above the ranger station. There is usually a designated camp across from the ranger station. The prominent peak visible from the trail is Hellroaring Mountain, one of the park's few exposed granite peaks.

True to its name, Hellroaring Creek is often high until mid-July. Hellroaring Creek (and trail) continue beyond the park boundary into Montana's beautiful Absaroka Primitive Area (where a Montana fishing license is required).

Average size of the cutthroat is about nine inches, with landing rates over one fish per hour. Angler satisfaction with over-all experience on the creek is excellent, especially for those who hike to the upper stretches.

Indian Creek

A tributary of the Gardner River, flowing close to a campground, with special regulations that allow children eleven and under to use worms as bait.

The most popular access is near the campground and the creek's confluence with the Gardner River. It can also be fished upstream by way of the east end of the Big Horn Pass Trail. The trail heads near Indian Creek Campground, crossing the mountains between Bannock and Antler peaks, and eventually following the Gallatin River headwaters. Fishing in Indian is rated above average for seven-inch brook trout, though it receives considerable angling pressure due to the proximity of the campground. Angler satisfaction with size of fish caught is below average, but anglers generally land one fish per hour.

Joffe Lake

An old reservoir located several miles south of the town of Mammoth. Access is by way of the Mammoth-Norris Grand Loop Road, 1.3 miles south of Mammoth. Turn onto the dirt road heading south to the lake.

Joffe contains brook trout averaging seven inches. Anglers rate their over-all experience on the lake excellent, but report below average satisfaction with size of fish caught.

Landslide Creek (See Reese Creek.)

Lava Creek

A tributary of the Gardner River, joining Gardner east of Mammoth. It contains primarily small brook trout, with a few rainbow and brown trout in the lower stream.

The lower creek is paralleled for several miles by the Grand Loop Road east of Mammoth, then is crossed by the road. Anglers also hike up Lava to fish its tributary, Arrow Canyon Creek. The fishing satisfaction rating for Lava Creek is excellent for the over-all experience, above average for the numbers of fish caught, and average for size of fish. Landing rate is one fish per hour, with fish averaging nine to ten inches.

Little Buffalo Creek

Offers good fishing for small cutthroat trout. It can be reached by taking the Garnet Hill Trail from Tower Junction, crossing the Yellowstone, then following the Buffalo Plateau Trail for one mile. A trail cutting off to the right crosses Little Buffalo Creek in another mile.

Lost Creek

A well regarded brook trout stream, tributary of Elk Creek in the Tower Junction area. The lower stretch of Lost Creek is accessed by the Garnet Hill Trail, which heads north from the Grand Loop Road west of Tower Junction. The stream joins Elk Creek after about two miles. Angler ratings indicate average satisfaction with Lost Creek's pan-size brook trout, with a landing rate approaching four fish per hour.

Lupine Creek

Lupine Creek joins Lava Creek just south of the Grand Loop Road. It offers some fishing for pan-size brook trout, although the majority of the stream is fishless.

Maple Creek

A brook and brown trout stream which receives a migration of larger fish from Hebgen Dam in its lower stretch.

To reach Maple, follow Highway 191 north eight miles from West Yellowstone. Watch for a sign on the right, turning right at the sign and keeping right one mile until you reach the telephone line that marks the park boundary. At the boundary, a road to the left leads to the Duck Creek parking area. Car tracks to the right lead to Maple Creek.

Maps to the contrary, Maple Creek no longer joins Cougar Creek. Cougar now disappears into a meadow, and it is Maple that Highway 191 crosses. The Gneiss Creek trail crosses Maple Creek upstream, where there is often a designated campsite. The fish average six inches with landing rates below one fish per hour.

ELK NEAR GARDNER RIVER

Mol Heron Creek

A small creek formed partially by the outlet waters of Sportsman Lake.

To fish the creek, follow the Mol Heron Trail, which branches off the Sportsman Lake Trail east of the lake. For complete road and trail directions, see Sportsman Lake. Mol Heron has offered good fishing for pan-size cutthroat trout for those who are willing to make the hike.

Obsidian Creek

A good brook trout stream, with special regulations that allow children eleven and under to fish with worms as bait. Obsidian Creek parallels the Mammoth-Norris Road from the Grizzly Lake Trailhead to Indian Creek Campground. Near the campground, at Sevenmile Bridge, Obsidian enters the Gardner River.

The creek contains brook trout averaging seven inches, with most angling activity occurring below the confluence of Straight Creek (outlet for Grizzly Lake). A lot of fish are caught here, and

OBSIDIAN CREEK

anglers report above average overall satisfaction with the experience and numbers of fish caught. Satisfaction with size of the fish is usually rated below average. Landing rates of over one fish per hour are often reported.

Oxbow Creek

A small mountain stream, tributary of the Yellowstone in the mid-Black Canyon stretch. It contains pan-size brook trout near its confluence with the Yellowstone, but is fishless upstream.

Panther Creek

A brook trout stream near Indian Creek Campground, with special regulations that allow children eleven and under to use worms as bait.

Panther flows into the Gardner River about one-half mile north of Indian Creek. The Big Horn Pass Trail follows the stream for several miles, providing access.

Panther offers fair fishing for brook trout averaging six inches. Anglers give this stream an average rating for over-all experience and numbers of fish caught, a below average rating for size of fish caught.

COYOTES ARE OFTEN SEEN IN THE PARK

Quartz Creek

A small mountain stream which flows into the Yellowstone from Specimen Ridge southeast of Tower Falls. Recent stream surveys suggest it offers marginal habitat and limited fisheries potential.

Reese Creek

A tributary of the Yellowstone River, joining the Yellowstone north of Gardiner where the Yellowstone River forms part of the park boundary. A park road heading north from Gardiner provides access to the stream.

Reese supports a small population of cutthroat and brown trout. At this time it is being closely monitored to determine ways to protect the fishery from irrigation withdrawals. Minimum flows have been established and fish screens installed but the problem has not been totally resolved. Nearby Stephens and Landslide creeks are similar, but catch data is unavailable.

Ribbon Lake

A rainbow trout lake in the scenic Grand Canyon area, offering rather difficult fishing from its marshy edge. The beautiful Ribbon Lake Trail begins at Artist Point, at the end of the Upper Falls spur road south of Canyon Village. The trail follows the rim of the Grand Canyon, within sight of several handsome peaks (Mt. Washburn, Dunraven Peak, and Hedges Peak from right to left), then moves into forest, past odiferous Lilypad Lake, to a junction with the Clear Lake Trail. Ribbon is to the left. Total mileage to Ribbon is two miles.

Ribbon Lake is about eleven acres, with maximum depth nineteen feet. It offers fishing for small rainbow trout averaging seven inches. The majority of anglers rate their experience here as average and are satisfied with the numbers of fish caught, though satisfaction with the size of fish is below average.

Richards Creek (See Duck Creek.)

Richards Pond

A small brook trout pond, headwaters of Richards Creek, a tributary of Duck Creek. It contains a healthy population of brook trout that can provide good angling success. See Duck Creek for directions to Richards. Follow Richards upstream.

Slide Lakes

A marginal rainbow trout fishery, formed when mudslides dammed a small creek that drained the Mammoth Beaver Ponds. The lakes are located three miles north of Mammoth and approximately one-third mile east of the old one-way dirt road from Mammoth to Gardiner. The trout population is concentrated primarily in the smaller lake. This is a marginal habitat, and the catch rate is slow.

Specimen Creek

A small stream, tributary of the Gallatin River, that offers fair fishing for cutthroat trout to ten inches. It can be fished by way of the Sportsman Lake Trail, which heads at the campground east of Highway 191 near the confluence of Specimen and the Gallatin, about twenty-seven miles north of West Yellowstone.

The creek forks at about 1 1/4 miles, with trails leading up each of the forks. The lower two miles of the Sportsman Lake Trail are very scenic, with big meadows and mountain vistas. Angler surveys indicate average satisfaction with their fishing experiences here, with landing rates approaching one fish per hour.

Specimen Creek, East Fork

One of two source streams for Specimen Creek, containing pan-size cutthroat trout. It is fed by fishless Crag and High lakes on the north flank of Meldrum Mountain.

To fish the East fork, follow the Sportsman Lake Trail along Specimen Creek about 1 1/4 miles, crossing the stream and bearing right (due east) at the trail fork. To continue to the headwaters at High Lake, bear left (north) at the Sportsman Lake junction. Recent stream surveys suggest the east fork may have a greater distribution of fish than the North Fork.

Specimen Creek, North Fork

Heads at Crescent Lake on the north flank of Meldrum Mountain. To fish the stream for its pan-size cutthroat, bear left (north) at the confluence of the east and north fork streams. The North Fork Trail follows the stream to its headwaters at Crescent Lake.

Sportsman Lake

A scenic four acre cutthroat lake that offers fishing for trout averaging ten inches. It sits at an elevation of 7730 feet, with a maximum depth of twenty-six feet.

Sportsman is accessed by the Sportsman Lake Trail, which heads west from the Grand Loop Road about 2 1/2 miles south of Mammoth, reaching the lake in eleven miles. The west end of the trail can be picked up at Specimen Creek, twenty miles north of West Yellowstone off Highway 191. The hike up Specimen Creek is especially attractive, past aspen groves and scenic meadows.

Anglers have given Sportsman Lake excellent ratings for the experience and numbers of fish caught. They report a landing rate of over four fish per hour.

Stellaria Creek

A tributary of the East Fork Fan Creek, north of the Fawn Pass Trail. Recent stream surveys indicate an absence of catchable trout.

Stephens Creek   (See Reese Creek.)

Straight Creek

A well regarded brook trout stream, flowing into the south end of Grizzly Lake and out the north end of the lake.

Below Grizzly Lake, Straight Creek is joined by Winter Creek approximately two miles from the Mount Holmes Trailhead on the Grand Loop Road. The Grizzly Lake Trail provides access to both streams.

Both creeks contain brook trout averaging seven inches. Anglers have rated the fishing excellent in all categories (experience, size and numbers). Landing rates of over two fish per hour have been reported.

Tower Creek

Offers good fishing for brook and rainbow trout in the Tower Falls Campground area. A trail heading southwest from the campground follows the creek upstream to its junction with Carnelian Creek.

The catch average is under nine inches, with the size of the fish decreasing the higher you fish. The landing rate is over one fish per hour. Angler satisfaction is rated excellent in all categories.

Trilobite Lake

A brook trout lake, unnamed on most maps, located at the western end of Winter Creek Meadow along the Mt. Holmes Trail. Little information is available regarding angler success. Recent surveys reported landing rates of over six fish per hour with the fish averaging over ten inches.

White Lake

Headwaters for Broad Creek. Originally thought to be barren of fish, recent aquatic surveys have revealed a developing cutthroat fishery. Access to the lake is by way of the Astringent Creek and the Pelican Creek trails. Pelican Creek trailhead is at the end of the service road about three miles from Fishing Bridge on the East Entrance Road.

Winter Creek (See Straight Creek.)

Yellowstone River (Inspiration Point to north boundary)

One of America's largest, wildest, and best trout streams, flowing a total of seventy miles. This portion of the river includes the Grand Canyon of the Yellowstone as well as the lower Black Canyon.

The Grand Canyon of the Yellowstone offers challenging fishing for some of the river's biggest fish. The number of anglers willing to make the 1500 foot descent is on the increase. Angler use of the Canyon stretch has doubled since 1976, and fish per hour landing rates have declined from almost four trout per hour to around one.

The most popular portion of the canyon is between Inspiration Point and Quartz Creek, where the river is accessed by the Seven Mile Hole Trail and Howard Eaton Trail. Seven Mile Hole Trail is especially scenic, heading near the Glacial Boulder above Canyon Village Campground. There is ample parking, and the trail is easy to find and well maintained.

The Grand Canyon is steep and the water swift, so caution is advised. Plan on a vigorous outing if you intend to go in and out the same day. When the stonefly hatch is on, the fish can literally wear you out. In this section, the Yellowstone can seldom be crossed by wading except

GROUND SQUIRREL

during low water, and then only in a few places. The river emerges from the canyon near Tower Falls (and campground), powerful and fast, but fishable.

Within a couple of miles, the Yellowstone enters the Black Canyon, which extends for twenty miles. Though less spectacular than the Grand, it is easier to access—more of a hike through sagebrush and juniper (one to four miles) than a climb. Wear good hiking boots, however, and leave your waders behind. Black Canyon water includes a challenging fast-water mix of runs and rapids, numerous cascades, and a full-blown falls, as well as some big deep pools. Cutthroat trout predominate here, though there are also rainbow, brook trout, and whitefish. The average size of the fish varies between twelve and fifteen inches, weighing one to two pounds. Fishing is rated good to excellent, with best catches in the less accessible stretches.

The most consistently successful flies used here match the stonefly nymphs which are found in the stream year around. Bring a variety of sizes, both black and gold. Dry flies can also be effective, especially during the salmonfly hatches from June to September. This portion of the river can be reached by several trails, including the Yellowstone River Trail, Blacktail Trail and Garnet Hill Trail. For information about these and other fishing trails into this area, inquire at Tower Junction. Anglers fishing the canyons should consider carrying a sleeping bag, extra rations, and the necessary permits, just in case good fishing draws you further from the road than originally planned.

The lower section of the Yellowstone, between Knowles Falls and the north park boundary, contains cutthroat, rainbow, brown, and brook trout as well as whitefish, with some catches over eighteen inches. To access this stretch, follow the Yellowstone River Trail which heads at Gardiner (North Entrance), the Blacktail Trail from the Grand Loop Road east of Mammoth, or the park road following the boundary north from Gardiner.

Over-all satisfaction with the Yellowstone River is currently above average to excellent in all categories. The average length of fish landed has increased to over fifteen inches.

YELLOWSTONE RIVER

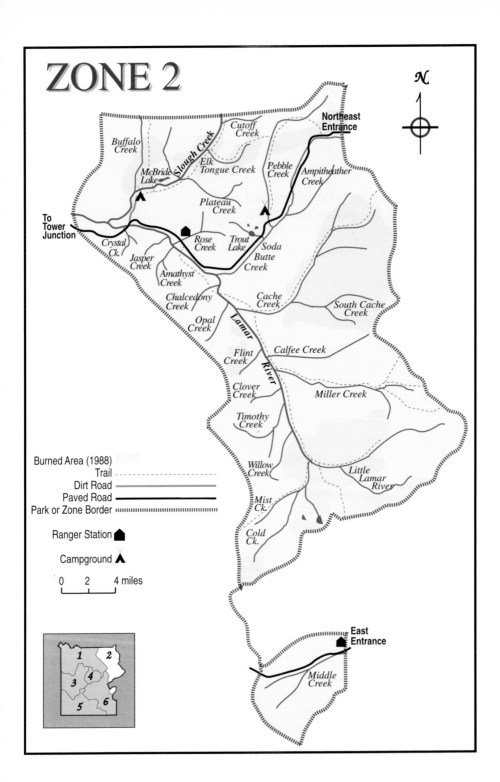

ZONE 2

Buffalo Creek
McBride Lake
Slough Creek
Cutoff Creek
Northeast Entrance
Elk Tongue Creek
Pebble Creek
Ampitheather Creek
Plateau Creek
To Tower Junction
Crystal Ck.
Jasper Creek
Rose Creek
Trout Lake
Soda Butte Creek
Amathyst Creek
Chalcedony Creek
Cache Creek
South Cache Creek
Opal Creek
Lamar River
Flint Creek
Calfee Creek
Clover Creek
Miller Creek
Timothy Creek
Willow Creek
Little Lamar River
Mist Ck.
Cold Ck.
East Entrance
Middle Creek

Burned Area (1988)
Trail
Dirt Road
Paved Road
Park or Zone Border

Ranger Station
Campground

0 2 4 miles

N

1 2
3 4
5 6

ZONE 2

The Lamar River and Middle Creek watersheds east of Sylvan Pass.

This is an area of rugged mountains and wide open valleys. The Lamar River is the central feature, collecting water from a vast wilderness area. It is best fished after the early summer snow melt. The Lamar is easily influenced by storms, which cause discoloration and poor fishing.

Slough Creek, a tributary of the lower Lamar, is a favorite of park anglers. It flows through a broad grassy meadow within easy hiking of the Northeast Entrance Road.

The scenery in this area is outstanding even by Yellowstone standards, with the Beartooth Range and Absaroka peaks dominating the view. Elk, bison, antelope, and deer winter here, and spring and fall are good seasons for wildlife watching. Mosquitoes thrive in these meadows and valleys usually until late July.

This zone is reached via the Northeast Entrance Road between the entrance and Tower. The Middle Creek watershed is accessed by the Grand Loop Road from Fishing Bridge to East Entrance Road. There are campgrounds at Slough Creek and Pebble Creek.

Amphitheater Creek

A tributary of Soda Butte Creek near Pebble Creek Campground. It offers limited fishing for cutthroat averaging eleven inches. Amphitheater flows into Soda Butte Creek about one mile above the campground. Thunderer Cutoff Trail begins almost at the confluence, heading west across The Thunderer Mountain. Landing rates of over one fish per hour are reported.

Buffalo Creek

A tributary of Slough Creek, offering good fishing for cutthroat averaging eleven inches. Buffalo Creek empties into Slough Creek near the campground. Landing rates of over four fish per hour have been achieved.

Cache Creek

A major tributary of the Lamar River, offering above average fishing for cutthroat trout averaging twelve inches. The Cache Creek Trail follows the stream to its headwaters and beyond, crossing the Absaroka Range at Republic Pass. The trail heads northeast from the Lamar River Trail a little more than three miles beyond the Soda Butte Creek Bridge. The first two miles are carved into the hillside high above Cache Creek. The trail descends to Cache near Wahb Springs, which emits a noxious hydrogen sulphide gas and should be avoided. Landing rates of over one fish per hour are reported.

Cache Creek, South

A good tributary of Cache Creek. Anglers have reported excellent satisfaction with over-all experience here and number of fish caught, and above average satisfaction with size of fish. Landing rates of over two fish per hour have been reported.

SLOUGH CREEK BELOW THE CAMPGROUND

Calfee Creek

Enters the Lamar from the northeast about four miles beyond the Cache Creek Trail cut-off. Anglers have given Calfee excellent ratings in all categories for its cutthroat fishery, with the fish averaging nine inches..

Chalcedony Creek

A tributary of the Lamar, lightly fished for pan-size cutthroat near its mouth. It is crossed by the Lamar River Trail just northwest of the Specimen Ridge Trail.

Clover Creek

Joins the Lamar River between Miller and Timothy confluences. It may maintain a small population of cutthroat trout.

Cold Creek

A good creek for hike-in anglers. Cold Creek enters the Lamar from the south, just a few miles from the end of the Lamar River Trail. It offers good fishing for ten-inch cutthroat, with reported landing rates of over one fish per hour.

There used to be some excellent campsites near the Cold Creek/Lamar confluence. The Cold Creek patrol cabin is on the Lamar about 1/2 mile before the Cold Creek confluence, at the junction of the Mist Creek Trail.

Crystal Creek

A small stream flowing into the Lamar River near the crossing of the Northeast Entrance Road, about four miles east of Tower Junction. Crystal supports a population of pan-size cutthroat.

Elk Tongue Creek

A tributary of Slough Creek crossed by the Slough Creek Wagon Trail, which heads northeast from Slough Creek campground. Small cutthroat trout are available near the Elk Tongue Patrol Cabin. Further upstream the creek has few fish.

Flint Creek

Flint Creek flows into the Lamar from the southwest about 4 miles south of the Cache Creek Trail, just upstream from the Calfee Creek confluence. It offers fishing for pan-size cutthroat.

Lamar River

One of the longest rivers in the park, tributary of the Yellowstone, a popular fishery for good size cutthroat and rainbow trout. The most accessible stretch receives considerable angling pressure.

The Northeast Entrance Road follows the Lamar for over seven miles east to the mouth of Soda Butte Creek. This is the most popular stretch of the river, where the water flows relatively slower through a meadow valley prior to entering its canyon. There are large fish in the canyon's pocket water for anglers who like fast water fishing.

From the Soda Butte confluence upstream anglers must hit the trail. The Lamar River Trail begins on the southeast side of the Northeast Entrance Road about eight miles from Tower Junction. It follows the river closely right into the headwaters in the Absaroka Range. Most of the way is heavily wooded. Side trails follow Cache Creek and Miller Creek, both of which offer excellent fishing. If the

LAMAR RIVER VALLEY

upper Lamar is your destination, be aware that there is no bridge across Cache Creek, which can run high throughout June. Buffalo are often sighted in the area.

Best fished later in the summer, the Lamar River is one of the last streams to clear following spring runoff, and it is often discolored by local thunder storms. Cache, Miller, and Soda Butte creeks are all good alternatives when the Lamar is too muddy to fish.

Fishermen rate the Lamar excellent to above average for over-all experience and size of fish. Above average ratings are usual for the number of fish. Landing rates are above one fish per hour. Angler success and the average size of trout landed has increased since the implementation of catch and release regulations in portions of the river.

Little Lamar River

Near the end of the Lamar River Trail, joining the Lamar about a mile from the Cold Creek Patrol Cabin. See Cold Creek for additional information.

The Little Lamar has offered fair fishing for pan-size cutthroat trout.

McBride Lake

A beautiful twenty-three acre lake situated in grizzly country off the Slough Creek Trail. It offers excellent fishing for cutthroat trout averaging about fourteen inches before a late summer algal bloom slows the action. You will need a topographic map to find it.

To reach McBride, follow the Slough Creek Wagon Trail northeast from Slough Creek Campground. The old road climbs through forest for about two miles before reaching Slough Creek in its meadow setting. McBride is above the meadow to the northeast. This bushwhack includes a fording of Slough Creek, which can be high and fast throughout June. McBride Lake is closed to camping due to the presence of bears.

Anglers report landing rates approaching three fish per hour and excellent satisfaction with McBride in all survey categories.

Middle Creek

A good trout stream, accessed by the East Entrance Road throughout much of its run through the park. If you are heading east toward the entrance after leaving Yellowstone Lake, you will spot Middle Creek on the right just after crossing Sylvan Pass.

Middle Creek supports rainbow and cutthroat trout averaging eleven inches in length. Anglers report excellent satisfaction with over-all fishing experience here, above average satisfaction with number caught and size of fish landed. Landing rates are over one fish per hour.

Miller Creek

Tributary of the Lamar, offering excellent fishing for cutthroat trout. The Miller Creek Trail heads east off the Lamar River Trail about a mile southeast of Calfee Creek, following Miller to its headwaters below Hoodoo Peak in the Absaroka Range. Anglers report landing rates approaching two fish per hour and excellent satisfaction with their over-all experience. The fish average eleven inches in length.

Mist Creek

A tributary of Cold Creek, supporting a population of cutthroat averaging thirteen inches. The Mist Creek Trail cuts south off the Lamar River Trail at Cold Creek, following Mist through Mist Creek Pass then continuing down into Pelican Valley. . The Cold Creek patrol cabin is located about 1/2 mile before the Cold Creek confluence on the west side of the Lamar.

Opal Creek

A tributary of the Lamar River, occasionally fished for pan-size cutthroat near its mouth. Access is by way of the Lamar River Trail, about a mile southeast of the Soda Butte crossing.

Pebble Creek

A good trout fishery near Pebble Creek Campground, 9 1/2 miles from the Northeast Entrance. Pebble Creek Trail follows the creek north, eventually looping back to the Northeast Entrance Road, just 1 1/2 miles inside the park.

Pebble Creek contains cutthroat and rainbow trout averaging ten inches, with a landing rate approaching two fish per hour. It is awarded excellent angler ratings for over-all experience, and size and number of fish caught. The upper waters of the creek support a good trout population, though of smaller size.

The Pebble Creek Trail provides vistas of some of the park's most spectacular scenery.

Rose Creek

A cutthroat stream crossed by the Northeast Entrance Road near the Lamar Ranger Station. The fish average six inches in length, with reported landing rates exceeding six fish per hour.

Slough Creek

A fine cutthroat fishery and beautiful stream in a splendid setting. Slough is a major tributary of the Lamar River, joining it about three miles east of Tower Junction.

A spur road off the Northeast Entrance Road about four miles east of Tower Junction leads north to Slough Creek Campground. From the campground, the Slough Creek Wagon Trail follows the stream to the park boundary, though hikers heading for First Meadow are advised to begin their trek from the trailhead on the north side of the entrance road, east of the campground, in order to avoid a steep, difficult piece of trail.

Throughout most of its flow through the park, Slough Creek is a slow moving meadow stream, supporting cutthroat, rainbow and hybrid trout that average twelve to fifteen inches. The lower

FIRST MEADOW, SLOUGH CREEK

section, however, from the Lamar confluence to just above the campground, is characterized by riffles and cascades. It is easy to access on foot and supports larger fish, but offers a lower catch rate for its more prevalent rainbow and rainbow hybrids. Slough Creek above the Cascades, near the campground, is a pure cutthroat fishery.

The First Meadow stretch of Slough, a one-mile hike from the trailhead, is extremely peaceful, offering smaller but respectable cutthroat and a catch rate higher than that of the Yellowstone's Hayden Valley.

In the Second Meadow section of Slough, two hours further up the trail, the creek meanders through an alpine valley with views of the peaks of the Absaroka, Beartooth, and Washburn ranges.

Anglers have given Slough an excellent rating for fish caught in the less accessible areas, and for size of fish landed. The average size of fish in this stream is increasing as a result of catch and release regulations.

Soda Butte Creek

A very nice trout stream in a lovely valley, easily accessed throughout its park run by the Northeast Entrance Road between the entrance gate and the creek's confluence with the Lamar River.

Soda Butte offers fishing for cutthroat trout averaging over ten inches. Angler surveys on Soda Butte Creek indicate excellent satisfaction with the over-all experience, above average satisfaction with size and number of fish caught. The landing rate is over one fish per hour.

Timothy Creek

Joins the Lamar River from the south about 2 1/2 miles upstream from the Miller Creek Trail junction. It offers fishing for pan-size cutthroat in its lower reaches.

Trout Lake

Heavily fished for rainbow and cutthroat, Trout Lake is located about one mile southwest of the Pebble Creek Campground, close to the Northeast Entrance Road. Watch for a vehicle turn-out on the west side of the road. There is no sign.

A half-mile trail leads to the lake, which is partially surrounded by hilly meadows that attract grazing buffalo. Mt. Hornaday is to the north.

Trout Lake receives heavy angling pressure, with catches averaging sixteen inches. Recent surveys indicate a landing rate of less than one fish per hour. Anglers give an above excellent rating to number of fish caught, size of fish landed, and to the over-all experience here.

Willow Creek

Enters the Lamar River from the south, about four miles upstream from the Miller Creek Trail junction. It offers fishing for cutthroat in its lower reaches that average six inches. Landing rates that approach three fish per hour have been reported.

SODA BUTTE CREEK

WILLOW CREEK

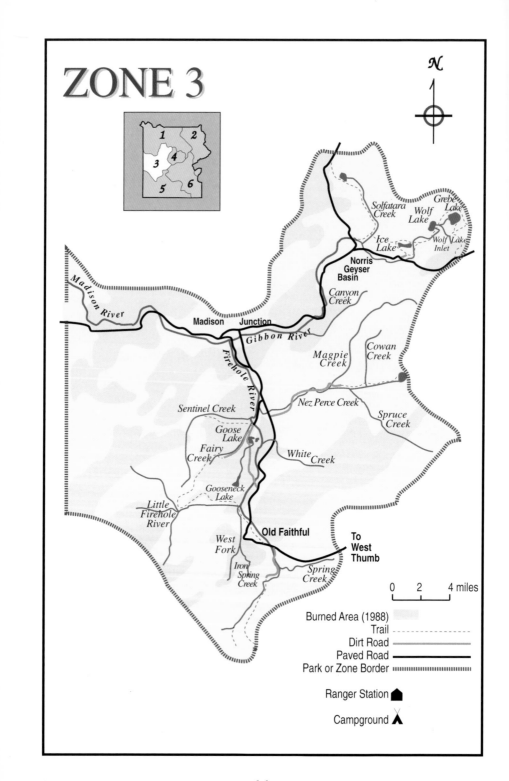

ZONE 3

N

1	2
3	4	
5	6

Grebe
Lake
Solfatara
Creek
Wolf
Lake
Ice
Lake
Wolf Lake
Inlet

Madison River

**Norris
Geyser
Basin**

Canyon
Creek

Madison   Junction

Gibbon River

Magpie
Creek

Cowan
Creek

Firehole River

Nez Perce Creek

Spruce
Creek

Sentinel Creek

Goose
Lake

Fairy
Creek

White Creek

Gooseneck
Lake

Little
Firehole
River

Old Faithful

**To
West
Thumb**

West
Fork

Iron
Spring
Creek

Spring
Creek

0   2   4 miles

Burned Area (1988)
Trail
Dirt Road
Paved Road
Park or Zone Border

Ranger Station
Campground

- 66 -

ZONE 3

Headwaters of the Madison River, including the Gibbon and Firehole River watersheds.

This zone is dominated by the Gibbon and Firehole Rivers, which join in National Park Meadow to create the Madison, of which a fourteen-mile segment flows within Yellowstone Park.

The waters of the Firehole are warmed by numerous geothermal features, including Old Faithful and many lesser known geysers and springs. Bison and elk spend the entire year in the Firehole Valley and are sometimes seen in large numbers here.

The Gibbon River heads at Grebe Lake, where an angler willing to make the hike can still catch a grayling. Gibbon Meadows is usually home to an elk herd, and is a prime location for wildlife viewing.

The three major rivers of this zone are easily accessed by roads which parallel each of the streams. The West Entrance Road follows the Madison to Madison Junction, then tracks the Gibbon to Norris Geyser Basin. The Grand Loop Road follows the Firehole south from Madison Junction to Old Faithful.

Accommodations in this area are available at West Yellowstone outside the park, and at Old Faithful within the park. There are campgrounds at Madison Junction and Norris.

Canyon Creek

A tributary of the Gibbon River, joining the river below Gibbon Falls.

The stream was chemically treated in 1975 to remove all species of fish so that grayling could be restored to this watershed. A barrier was constructed to prevent other fish from returning to the area. The project hoped to establish a self-perpetuating grayling fishery similar to the original fishery in this watershed. Either trout surmounted the barrier or the chemical treatment was not successful and the grayling project was discontinued due to expanding trout populations and poor grayling survival rate. Today the river supports populations of small brown and rainbow trout, that average six inches in length with reported landing rates of over two fish per hour.

Cowan Creek

A tributary of Nez Perce Creek, entering the stream from the north. It offers fair fishing for small brook, brown, and rainbow trout.

Fairy Creek

Tributary of the Firehole, joining the river in the Lower Basin along Fountain Flats Freight Road. It supports populations of rainbow, brown, and brook trout, offering fair fishing for trout that average almost eight inches.

During hot weather, it will contain larger fish that are seeking refuge in the cooler creek waters. These refugees are usually very wary and hard to catch. Angler satisfaction is above average for all categories except size of fish, which received average ratings.

Firehole River

One of the most popular fly fishing streams in the Park, flowing more than thirty miles from Madison Lake near the Continental Divide, through the Upper Geyser Basin, to a rendezvous with the Gibbon River at Madison Junction near West Yellowstone.

MULESHOE BEND ON THE FIREHOLE RIVER

Much of the Firehole's best water is followed closely by the Grand Loop Road between Madison Junction and Old Faithful. The river supports populations of rainbow, browns, brook trout, and whitefish. The average size of the catch has dropped to ten inches in recent years, but some fish exceed eighteen inches.

The Firehole is subject to many geothermal influences, which cause fluctuating temperatures and, at times, poor fishing. In places you can feel the hot water seep around your feet while wading. During July and August, many trout leave the Firehole for the cooler water of its tributaries. Iron Spring Creek is especially attractive to the river's big browns and rainbow.

The river is no longer quite as impressive as it was when Ray Bergman wrote so eloquently of it in his classic, *Trout*, and larger trout now seem to prefer the lower river. But the fish still rise like clockwork to infinitesimal insects at Muleshoe Bend.

Access to the Firehole is readily available from the highway, with fishing trails following the banks wherever the stream wanders away from the road. Firehole regulars have many favorite holes and runs. Heading upstream from Madison Junction, take the scenic loop to reach the fast-water fishing of the Firehole Canyon. The canyon contains good-size fish, including some of the big trout that migrate up the Madison in the fall. Above the canyon, in the Lower Basin, Fountain Flats Freight Road follows the Firehole while the main road veers away. The water through this area offers choice dry fly fishing for the expert angler. Keep an eye out for marshy banks.

Fountain Flats Road continues to Goose and Feather lakes, where it dead ends. Upstream from this point, the stream narrows and offers some good, deep runs and riffles. At the upper end of Mid-way Geyser Basin is the famous Muleshoe Bend, a half mile of prime water for big trout. From the Mid-way Basin up to Morning Glory Pool there is good dry fly water.

The Little Firehole River and Iron Spring Creek enter the river in Biscuit Basin, offering refuge for trout when the Firehole hits eighty degrees in the heat of summer. The basin includes excellent dry fly water. Above Kepler Cascades, where the Grand Loop Road veers away from the river toward the West Thumb of Yellowstone Lake,

FISHING NEXT TO A FIREHOLE HOT SPRING

the Firehole is a typical mountain stream, shallow, with many riffles and few holes. Fishing pressure on the Firehole is heavy and the fish wary, so angler success can range from poor to excellent, depending on skill. Recent landing rates for this stream are reported to be under one fish per hour. Angler satisfaction with the over-all experience is excellent and above average for the number caught and size landed. July and August are considered poor months to fish the river.

Gibbon River

A fine trout stream, flowing 38 miles from its headwaters in lovely Grebe Lake to its rendezvous with the Firehole at Madison Junction, where the two join to form the Madison River. From Gibbon Falls to its confluence, the Gibbon is restricted to fly fishing only.

The Gibbon is easily accessed by the Norris Canyon Road, which follows the river from its confluence to Virginia Meadows.

Brown and brook trout, averaging eight inches, are the primary fishery. Rainbow, cutthroat and whitefish are also found in portions of the river. The Virginia Meadows stretch above Virginia Cascades supports a good population of small brook trout. This mile-long meadow is a popular place to picnic and give youngsters a crack at flyfishing for pan-size brook trout.

The Gibbon remains a panfishery until it enters Elk Park below Norris Geyser Basin. Both the Elk Park and Gibbon Meadow flows can produce some surprisingly large trout. There are some nice pools at the lower end of Gibbon Meadows, but most of the meadow stretch is typical dry fly water. Don't forget to bring grasshopper imitations for late summer fishing.

The pool below Gibbon Falls has been known to produce lunker trout, and the canyon stretch beyond the falls offers good fast-water fishing. The Gibbon and Firehole Rivers meet in National Park Meadow to form the Madison. The National Meadow stretch of the Gibbon offers good trout habitat, including many pools, weed beds, and undercut banks.

Angler surveys report nearly one fish per hour caught on the Gibbon. Anglers express above average satisfaction with their experience, average satisfaction with the number of fish caught, but give below average rating for the size of fish caught. The biggest catches are taken below Gibbon Falls, and catch size (and angler pressure) progressively decrease up river, though more fish are landed in the upper sections.

Goose Lake

A marginal fishery for rainbow trout averaging eleven inches.

The 34 acre lake is located immediately east of Fountain Flats Freight Road, about 5 1/2 miles south of Madison Junction. A picnic area beside the lake provides access, and there are other opportunities to drive down to the lake. Goose has a small inlet and no outlet stream.

Angler satisfaction with the experience here is average, below average for numbers caught, and above average for the size of the fish. Landing rates approaching one fish per hour are reported.

Gooseneck Lake

A small lake directly west of the Midway Geyser Basin. To reach it, follow directions to Goose Lake. The tributary that flows into the south end of Goose Lake is the Gooseneck Lake outlet. Follow the stream to Gooseneck. Gooseneck supports a population of rainbow trout that average eight inches.

Grebe Lake

Source of the Gibbon River, a big lake (156 acres) with a healthy population of rainbow trout and a catch and release fishery for plentiful grayling.

The lake can be reached by following the Ice Lake Trail north from Virginia Meadows. At Ice Lake, you can pick up the Howard Eaton Trail on Ice's north shore, and continue east past Wolf Lake to Grebe. A more direct route follows an old wagon road north from the Norris Canyon Road southwest of Canyon Village. Coming from the west, the old track cuts off less than a mile beyond a service road that branches off to the right. Grebe Lake, at elevation 8028 feet, is a very popular grayling fishery with good to excellent catches at times. The fish average eleven inches. Landing rates have been over one fish per hour. Anglers report excellent satisfaction with their experience and with number and size of fish caught.

Grebe is in grizzly country, so keep an eye out and make lots of noise on the trail.

Iron Spring Creek

A small creek that empties into the Little Firehole near Old Faithful, a favorite refuge of the Firehole River's big trout during summer hot spells. Cooler than the Little Firehole, it supports resident populations of rainbow, brook, and brown trout averaging

WORKING THE CUTBANKS ON THE MADISON RIVER

seven inches in length. When the Firehole approaches eighty degrees, many large fish move into this creek. They are extremely wary, however, and hard to catch.

Fishermen surveys indicate a landing rate approaching one fish per hour. Average ratings are reported for angler satisfaction with their experience, numbers caught, and with the size of the fish.

Little Firehole River

Tributary of the Firehole, entering the river just above the Biscuit Basin parking area, a mile or so below Old Faithful. Rainbow, brook, brown, and cutthroat trout averaging over eight inches offer anglers above average satisfaction with their over-all experience, with number of fish caught, and average for size of fish. Landing rates have been running over one fish per hour.

Madison River

Headwaters of one of the West's most famous fisheries. It is formed by the confluence of the Firehole and Gibbon rivers just fifteen miles inside the West Entrance of Yellowstone Park. The Madison then flows another 136 miles to Three Forks, Montana, where it meets the Gallatin and Jefferson to produce the Missouri River.

Easily accessed from the West Entrance Road throughout most of its National Park flow, it is heavily fished, though its wary and well-protected population elude many anglers who try their luck here. The Madison is restricted to fly fishing only.

Within the park the river supports large populations of brown trout, rainbow trout and whitefish, as well as some cutthroat and brook trout. The resident fish vary greatly in size, even in this relatively short stretch, with many browns and rainbow over three pounds, and some enormous whitefish. Even larger fish migrate from Hebgen Lake to spawn in the Madison, enhancing the fishing potential. There are spring and fall runs of rainbow, a fall run of whitefish, and a famous fall run of brown trout.

There is a large campground and parking lot at the head of the river, known as Madison Junction. The many vehicle turn-outs between the Junction and the Western Entrance usually indicate worthy fishing. Near the Junction, the Madison flows through National Park Meadows, an extremely weedy stretch with many big holes and runs that have been known to hold very big fish.

As with many rivers beloved of fishermen, the Madison's best holes and drifts are lovingly (though unofficially) named. The big elbow in the National Park Meadow stretch is known as Big Bend (site of a huge deep hole, best fished with heavy nymphs). Nine Mile Hole (nine miles from West Yellowstone, 4 1/2 miles from the entrance gate), is a very productive boulder-filled quarter mile stretch with deep water, gravel bars, and thick weed beds, best fished with dry flies. Downstream, (after a two mile flow between treacherously swampy banks) is Seven Mile Run, which begins just above the bridge. Seven Mile is characterized by weedy channels, downed trees, big boulders, and ledges that shelter many fish and make fishing for them extremely challenging.

Another excellent stretch of water is accessed by a side road that turns left six-tenths of a mile inside the Park. The road crosses a flat

MADISON ANGLERS (NOTE ELK ON FAR SHORE)

ELK ARE SURE-FOOTED WADERS

and ends at the Barns Holes. Traditional etiquette here is to fish the holes from head to tail. Cable Car Run is just above Barns Hole One. There are other unnamed holes beyond the Barns Holes.

In general anglers should plan on using small dry flies in the upper stretch and big nymphs in the Barns Holes area, where stone-flies predominate. Grasshopper imitations do well in the meadow areas from July through September. Waders are recommended for reaching the best holding water.

The above average to average satisfaction ratings reported by the majority of anglers fishing the park run of the Madison has more to do with angler skill and the difficulty of fishing for these wary and well educated trout in the river's clear waters than with trout avail-ability. Landing rates of under one fish per hour are reported. A spawning run from Hebgen Lake occurs in the fall, and is very popular with local anglers. Almost one-third of the fishing pressure on the river occurs during the fall.

Magpie Creek

A tributary of Nez Perce Creek, offering fair fishing for rainbow, brown, and brook trout. Magpie enters the Nez Perce from the north about five miles up the Mary Mountain Trail, which heads on the east side of the Grand Loop Road in the Lower Basin area. The trail crosses Magpie Creek just before its confluence with the Nez Perce. The fish average nine inches with reported landing rates under one fish per hour.

Nez Perce Creek

A tributary of the Firehole, joining the river from the east just downstream of Fountain Flats Freight Road. The Mary Mountain Trail follows the stream from confluence to source (Marys Lake, which contains no fish).

Nez Perce supports populations of brown, rainbow, and brook trout, but only offers marginal fishing. Above Cowan Creek the Nez Perce no longer sustains fish life due to high temperatures and acidic water.

Angler surveys indicate above average satisfaction with the overall experience here but below average with number of fish caught and with size of the fish. Landing rates are below one fish per hour.

Solfatara Creek

A tributary of the Gibbon, joining the river at Norris Junction near the Norris Ranger Station. Access is provided by the Solfatara Creek Trail, which begins near the station. There are fine meadows in the headwaters area.

Brook trout averaging six inches provide a landing rate of one fish per hour. Anglers give the creek an excellent rating for number of fish landed. Angler satisfaction with over-all experience and size of fish is average.

Spring Creek

Enters the Firehole River several miles east of Old Faithful. From the Grand Loop Road heading towards West Thumb, you will see Spring Creek, a small stream, on your right. It supports a small population of brook trout and a few brown trout averaging seven inches, with a landing rate of under one fish per hour.

Spruce Creek

A tributary of Nez Perce Creek, entering Nez Perce from the south about 1 1/2 miles upstream from the Magpie Creek confluence. It offers fair fishing for pan-size brook, brown, and rainbow trout.

West Fork

A small mountain stream that flows into Iron Spring Creek near its confluence with the Little Firehole. It contains rainbow and brown trout that average twelve inches in length, with reported landing rates of under one fish per hour.

White Creek

A small stream located along the Fountain Paint Pot scenic loop off the Grand Loop Road mid-way between Lower and Mid-way geyser basins. It has a population of brown trout that can provide some good fishing action.

Wolf Lake

Wolf Lake, attractively set among big meadows and pine forest, is a good rainbow and grayling fishery in the Gibbon River drainage, southwest of Grebe Lake. Wolf can be reached by way of the Howard Eaton Trail from trailheads on Norris Canyon Road or from the Grebe Lake Trail. Wolf Lake is in grizzly country, so keep an eye out.

The lake covers about fifty acres and is thirty-two feet deep. The Gibbon river both drains and sources the lake, and additional inlet streams on the north shore offer further fishing opportunities.

Anglers give Wolf an excellent rating for over-all experience and number of fish caught. Fish average over ten inches, with a landing rate of just under one fish per hour.

ZONE 4

ZONE 4

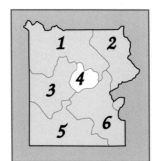

The Yellowstone River watershed from Inspiration Point to a point one mile downstream from the Yellowstone Lake Outlet.

Hayden Valley, a vast grazing area for bison, elk, moose, and grizzly bear, is a major feature of Zone 4. But the greatest attraction in this zone is the Yellowstone River and its cutthroat trout. Eighty percent of the fishing on the Yellowstone River takes place in this section.

The Yellowstone River is closed to fishing until July 15 to protect spawning cutthroat, so plan accordingly. From May through July the cutthroat congregate in pools below Le Hardy Rapids, about four miles downstream from the lake outlet. The rapids area is closed to fishing, but the trout are readily visible from a boardwalk and viewing platform at the site, and it is not unusual to see cutthroat attempting to jump the rapids.

The Grand Loop Road from the lake to Canyon follows the river closely, providing good access. Accommodations are available at Canyon Village and Lake Lodge. There are campgrounds at Bridge Bay, Fishing Bridge, and Canyon Village.

Alum Creek

Tributary of the Yellowstone, with a resident population of small cutthroat. It is currently closed to angling to protect spawning grounds. Alum is crossed by the Canyon-Fishing Bridge Road.

Bluff Creek

Tributary of Sour Creek. It is currently closed to angling to protect spawning grounds. It offers fair to good fishing for small cutthroat trout.

Bog Creek

Tributary of Sour Creek. It is currently closed to angling to protect spawning grounds. Like its neighbor, Bluff Creek, it offers fair to good fishing for small cutthroat trout.

Cascade Creek

Outlet of Cascade Lake, offering good fishing for cutthroat trout. See Cascade Lake for directions.

Cascade Creek cutthroat average ten inches. Angler surveys report above average satisfaction with over-all fishing experience and with number of fish caught, but only average satisfaction with size of fish. Cascade Lake offers catch-and-release fishing for cutthroat and grayling.

Cascade Lake

A popular lake in the Canyon Junction area, with catch-and-release fisheries for cutthroat trout and grayling. This area was burned during the fires of 1988. Check on the status of recovery before planning a trip.

There are two trails to the lake, each 2 1/2 miles long. The Cascade Creek Trail follows the lake's outlet stream (Cascade Creek) from a trailhead 1/2 mile west of Canyon Junction. A second trail heads at the picnic area about one mile north of Canyon Junction. Cascade Creek Trail offers the more scenic route.

The lake covers thirty-six acres, with a maximum depth of twenty-seven feet. There is a small inlet stream at the east end of the lake in a heavily forested area. The inlet is a gathering place for spawning grayling in early June.

Cascade receives very heavy angling pressure, but yields over one fish per hour. Anglers report excellent satisfaction with over-all experience, and above average satisfaction with size and number of fish landed. Catch-and-release management has increased angler satisfaction ratings in all categories.

Cascade is in grizzly country. Hikers are advised to inquire at a ranger station for reports of bear sightings, travel in groups of four or more, and obey bear area precautions.

Cottongrass Creek

A small tributary of the Yellowstone entering the river from the east and crossed by the Howard Eaton Trail. It supports a resident population of pan-size cutthroat, but is closed to angling to protect spawning grounds.

Elk Antler Creek

Tributary of the Yellowstone with a resident population of small cutthroat. It is currently closed to angling to protect spawning grounds. Elk Antler is crossed by the Canyon-Fishing Bridge Road.

Sour Creek

A good cutthroat stream crossed by the Howard Eaton Trail. It is currently closed to angling to protect spawning grounds. Trail about two miles from the trailhead near Canyon.

Thistle Creek

Tributary of the Yellowstone, entering the river from the east in the vicinity of Le Hardy Rapids. It is crossed by the Howard Eaton Trail. Thistle offers fair angling for pan-size cutthroat trout.

Trout Creek

Tributary of the Yellowstone with a resident population of small cutthroat. It is currently closed to angling to protect spawning grounds. Trout Creek is crossed by the Canyon-Fishing Bridge Road.

YELLOWSTONE RIVER BELOW LE HARDY RAPIDS

Yellowstone River

(Yellowstone Lake Outlet to Inspiration Point)

 The most popular stretch of the river, including 8.7 river miles open to fishing. This section of the Yellowstone is restricted to catch-and-release fishing only. The river is closed at Le Hardy Rapids, and through Hayden Valley from Sulphur Cauldron downstream to Alum Creek so that anglers will not disturb the wildlife there, and from Chittenden Bridge downstream to the Silver Cord Cascade.

There is immediate access to the west bank of the river from the Grand Loop Road between Canyon and Fishing Bridge. Anglers can reach the east side of the river by following the Howard Eaton Trail, which can be picked up at Fishing Bridge or Canyon. It is possible to wade in chest waders across the river at the Buffalo Ford picnic area. Buffalo Ford is also one of several sections on the river that are accessible for use by less-abled anglers.

The very popular stretch of the river between Fishing Bridge and the Sulphur Cauldron can provide outstanding fishing for cutthroat trout averaging over fifteen inches. When the river opens for fishing on the fifteenth of July, the stone fly hatch (which really excites the larger trout) is usually still in progress. Stone fly imitations often elicit smashing strikes, especially in the rapids. Many flies are lost trying to turn lunker cutthroat from the faster water. Watching an eighteen-inch cutthroat slowly rise to your fly can play havoc with your nerves. The trout sucks the fly in with a slurping noise, then violently lunges and heads for the safety of the faster currents. The memory of these powerful lunkers will bring you back to the Yellowstone year after year.

Be sure to carry a small, fine-meshed landing net to protect the fish (and also your fingers), since all fish must be released in this section. If you come later in the summer and plan to fly fish, be prepared to use fine tippets and small flies, as the trout will be wary and very selective in their feeding habits.

This section of the river accounts for 80% of the river's total angling activity. If you seek solitude for your angling experience, look elsewhere. Surveys give a landing rate of one fish per hour, with excellent satisfaction with the experience and size of fish caught, and above average satisfaction with number of fish landed.

The average size of fish taken from the Yellowstone in recent years is increasing, a tribute to current management practices. Data collected by the Fish and Wildlife Service suggests that cutthroat trout in this portion of the river may be captured an average of nine times during the season, which is probably why the fish get so darn smart by the end of summer.

From Alum Creek to Chittenden Bridge the river is more lightly fished and considerably less productive, though good catches have been taken here at times. Anglers fishing this stretch should be wary of the heavier current and proximity of the falls.

ZONE 5

All park waters on the west slope of the Continental Divide.

R ich in scenic and angling treasures, this zone includes three major lakes (Lewis, Shoshone, and Heart) and four rivers (Lewis, Bechler, Falls, and Snake).

Shoshone Lake is the largest backcountry lake in the lower forty-eight states, and the most popular backcountry destination in the park. Canoeists make the trip by way of the Lewis Channel, which connects Shoshone with Lewis Lake. Lewis is the third largest lake in Yellowstone.

Bechler, Falls, and Snake rivers are all hike-in fisheries. Bechler and Falls are in the park's far southwest corner, known as Cascade Corner. Here you will find twenty-one of the Park's forty-one waterfalls.

The elevation in this zone is lower, the climate wetter, the meadows thick with vegetation (and mosquitos). The Snake River area is summer home to a great many elk. There are extensive meadows, and vistas to the east of the jutting peaks of the Absarokas. Wildlife here is varied and plentiful, including bear, deer, elk, moose, sandhill cranes, and great blue herons.

The Bechler and Falls River areas are accessed by Cave Falls and Reclamation roads, east of Ashton, Idaho. The South Entrance Road approaches the Snake River and Lewis Lake. There are campgrounds at Lewis Lake and South Entrance.

ZONE 5

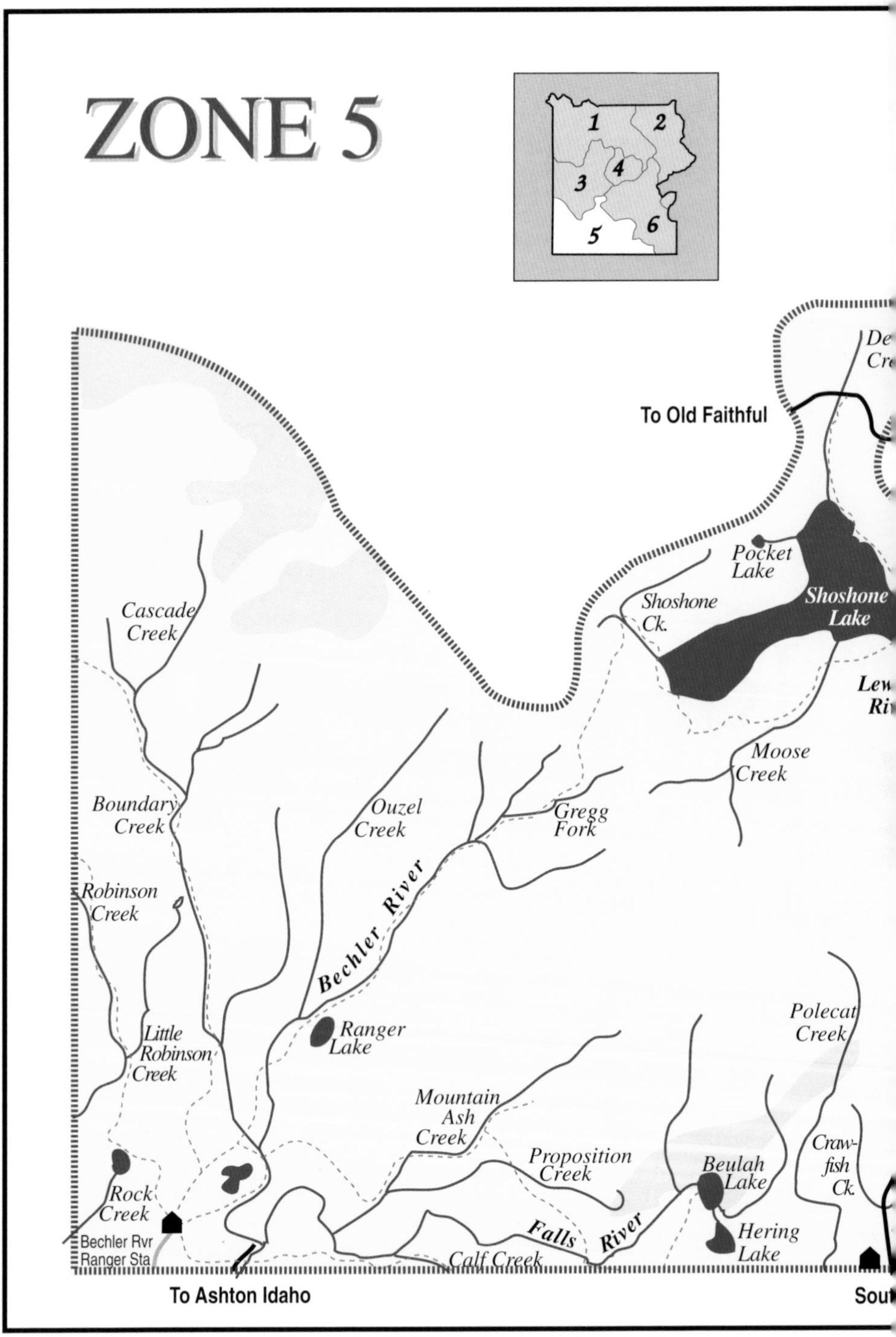

To Old Faithful

De
Cre

Pocket
Lake

Shoshone
Ck.

Shoshone
Lake

Lew
Riv

Cascade
Creek

Moose
Creek

Boundary
Creek

Ouzel
Creek

Gregg
Fork

Bechler River

Robinson
Creek

Polecat
Creek

Little
Robinson
Creek

Ranger
Lake

Mountain
Ash
Creek

Proposition
Creek

Beulah
Lake

Craw-
fish
Ck.

Rock
Creek

Bechler Rvr
Ranger Sta

Hering
Lake

Falls River

Calf Creek

To Ashton Idaho

Sout

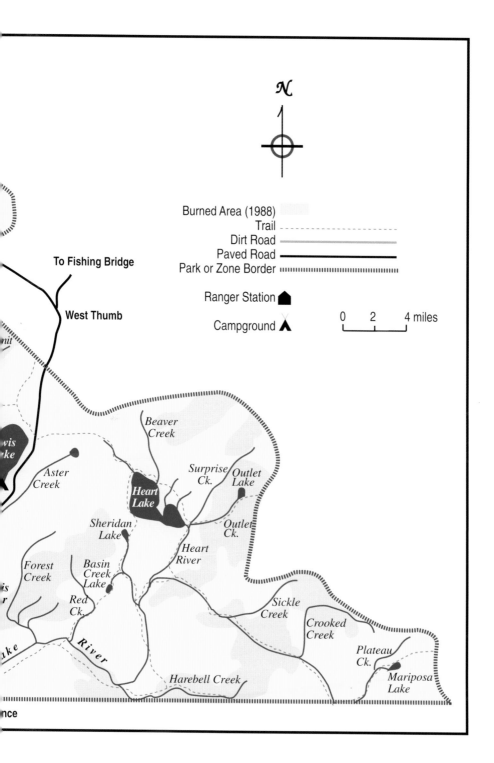

N

Burned Area (1988)
Trail
Dirt Road
Paved Road
Park or Zone Border

Ranger Station
Campground

0   2   4 miles

To Fishing Bridge

West Thumb

Beaver
Creek

Aster
Creek

Surprise
Ck.

Outlet
Lake

Heart
Lake

Sheridan
Lake

Outlet
Ck.

Heart
River

Forest
Creek

Basin
Creek
Lake

Red
Ck.

River

Sickle
Creek

Crooked
Creek

Plateau
Ck.

Mariposa
Lake

Harebell Creek

Aster Creek

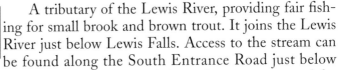

A tributary of the Lewis River, providing fair fishing for small brook and brown trout. It joins the Lewis River just below Lewis Falls. Access to the stream can be found along the South Entrance Road just below Lewis Lake. Catch rates of over two fish per hour are reported for trout that average six inches.

Basin Creek

An upper tributary of the Snake, fished for small cutthroat trout. Heart Lake Trail crosses the creek between Basin Creek Lake and Sheridan Lake. Other trails heading north from South Boundary Trail lead to the creek's lower waters.

Basin Creek Lake

A small lake on the west side of the Heart Lake Trail, about five miles south of Heart. It covers eight acres and has a maximum depth of seventeen feet. Its population of small cutthroat trout provides fair to good fishing.

Beaver Creek

Crossed by the Heart Lake Trail near Heart Lake's north shore, 1 1/2 miles east of Heart Lake Patrol Cabin. It supports a population of cutthroat trout. Anglers report a catch rate of over two fish per hour with an average length of nineteen inches.

Bechler River

A medium-size river, primarily a hike-in fishery for good sized cutthroat and rainbow trout. It joins Falls River at the end of Cave Falls Road. A trail follows the river from that point, eventually joining the Bechler River Trail, which heads at Bechler River Ranger Station.

To reach the main trailhead, take Highway 47 to Cave Falls

Road, then follow the ranger station cut-off. There is a parking lot for vehicles beside the trailhead.

The trail crosses a small stream and then forks at a pond (frequented by deer). Take the upper fork and, after about three miles of easy hiking, you will reach Bechler Meadows. To the north you can see Ouzel Falls. Moose, elk, deer, and sandhill cranes are frequently encountered in the upper meadow, and you may even get an opportunity to glimpse the rare whooping crane. Check the birder's logbook at the ranger station for latest sightings prior to hiking in.

The meadows area is usually very wet until late August, and the mosquitoes and flies can be thick. Be prepared.

Bechler's larger trout are found in the lower section of the river, from the upper meadows to the Falls River confluence. The average catch is about ten inches. Anglers often start fishing in the upper meadows where the trail crosses the river, then fish downstream to the confluence of Boundary Creek.

Bechler is clear and deep, requiring caution when wading. There are undercut banks and many deep holes that provide concealment for large trout. Bechler is a challenging river to fish, though it can provide good to excellent angling.

If you continue along Bechler River Trail from the upper meadows, you will enter the Bechler Canyon and soon reach Colonade Falls. There is a large pool beneath the falls that is worth fishing.

Angler success seems to have declined in recent years, and the frequency of large fish reports has decreased. However, anglers are still landing over one fish per hour, and surveys indicate above average satisfaction with over-all experience and size of fish landed. Satisfaction with numbers is below average. Most of the pressure on the river occurs in the Bechler Meadows area below Colonade Falls. Angler success is greater above the falls, but the fish are smaller.

Beula Lake

Headwaters of the Falls River, one of two nice backcountry cutthroat lakes near the park's south boundary. See also Hering Lake. Beula is approximately 107 acres, with a maximum depth of 36 feet.

The trail to Beula begins near the inlet of Grassy Lake in the Teton National Forest just south of the park. To reach the trailhead from the South Entrance, drive south to Reclamation Road (Ashton-Flagg), about two miles. The turn-off is near the Flagg Ranch by the Huckleberry Springs turn-off. This road is primitive and unmaintained, but passable for most passenger cars (not suitable for large RVs, however). Follow Reclamation Road to the tip of Grassy Lake. On your right you will find a limited vehicle parking area and an orange trail marker showing the trail head.

There are inlets on the north and south shores of the lake. The largest south shore inlet flows out of nearby Hering Lake.

Anglers give an excellent rating to Beula for over-all experience and number of fish caught. Size of fish landed is rated above average, with landing rates of over two fish per hour reported. Beula Lake fish average about eleven inches.

Boundary Creek

A tributary of the Bechler River, offering good fishing for cutthroat and rainbow trout. The upper waters of the creek are followed by Boundary Creek Trail (which leads to Buffalo Lake). A lower stretch can be accessed from the Bechler River Trail. This trail crosses Boundary just before its confluence with Bechler River at the lower end of Bechler Meadows. The meadows portion of either trail is usually very wet until later in the season (normally late August), and the mosquitoes and flies can be atrocious, so take plenty of repellent.

Boundary Creek contains cutthroat and rainbow trout that average almost nine inches, with landing rates of over two fish per hour. Anglers report above average satisfaction with over-all experience and with number of fish caught, average satisfaction with size.

The upper stretch of Boundary Creek includes the beautiful Dananda Falls, a 150 foot drop, and Silver Scarf Falls, a 250 foot cascade. There are also interesting geothermal features along the Boundary Creek Trail, and attractive wilderness vistas on the way to Buffalo Lake.

Calf Creek

A small stream accessed by the South Boundary Trail east of Cave Falls. It supports cutthroat and rainbow trout.

Cascade Creek

Tributary of Boundary Creek, supporting cutthroat and rainbow trout. Following the Boundary Creek Trail to the headwaters region, Cascade Creek is the first tributary to join Boundary Creek. Landing rates over three fish per hour have been reported for trout that average five inches in length.

Crawfish Creek

Crossed by the South Entrance Road just north of the entrance. It contains a small population of cutthroat trout offering fair fishing. Anglers report catch rates of nearly one fish per hour for trout that average over seven inches in length.

Crooked Creek

Tributary of the Snake River which drains the land east of Barlow Peak. It is reached by the Snake River Trail. Crooked joins the Snake from the north about three miles from the park's southern border. Small cutthroat trout provide fair to good fishing.

DeLacy Creek

An inlet of Shoshone Lake, with good fishing for brown and brook trout that average seven inches. A trail follows the creek all the way to Shoshone from a trailhead in DeLacy Park, just east of Craig Pass on the road between Old Faithful and West Thumb. Catch rates of over four fish per hour have been reported.

Falls River

A steeply flowing river, punctuated with many cascades, offering good to excellent fishing. It flows about thirty-one miles through the park's southwest boundary area. Bechler River joins Falls just above the dead-end Cave Falls Park Road. The best fishing requires a hike.

Access to Falls River is by way of the South Boundary Trail, which parallels the South Boundary of the park from the Idaho side of the park to the South Entrance. To reach the trailhead from the west, follow Reclamation Road on the Idaho side to Ashton, Idaho. At the east end of town, turn right onto Highway 32, then left at the Reclamation turn-off. About forty miles of dirt road leads to Flagg Ranch, which is located just outside the South Entrance to the Park. From the Wyoming side, the turn-off is marked by the Huckleberry Hot Springs sign just north of Flagg Ranch, where you will turn left and remain on the road towards Grassy Lake Reservoir. The road is primitive and poorly maintained, passable for most passenger cars, but not for large RVs. Seldom used, this road offers a very scenic view of the area. The headwaters of Falls River can also be approached from Beula Lake.

Angler success catching cutthroat and rainbow trout increases the further upstream you go, and the fishing pressure also decreases. Falls Creek is a popular stream with local fly anglers.

The frequency of catching larger trout, sixteen to twenty inches, appears to be declining, which may necessitate new regulations. Most recent angler surveys indicate a landing rate of almost three trout per hour, above average satisfaction with the over-all experience, average with the number of fish landed, and below average satisfaction with size of fish caught.

Forest Creek

A tributary of the Snake River that joins the Snake from the north about four miles along the South Boundary Trail that begins at the South Entrance. It supports a population of pan-size cutthroat trout that provide good fishing.

Gregg Fork

One of the headwaters of the Bechler River. It contains a population of cutthroat trout that average almost eleven inches. Landing rates over one fish per hour are not unusual.

Harebell Creek

Follows the South Boundary Trail in the vicinity of Harebell Patrol Cabin near the junction with Basin Creek Trail. It has a population of cutthroat trout.

Heart Lake

A large hike-in lake, with productive fisheries for cutthroat and lake trout, and some mountain whitefish. It covers about 2150 acres, with a maximum depth of 180 feet.

The Heart Lake Trailhead is on the east side of the South Entrance Road, just northeast of Lewis Lake (across from the Lewis-Shoshone Channel trailhead). The hike in is about eight miles, passing some interesting geothermal features.

Very large lake trout and some lunker cutthroat are caught here each year. The trout average over nineteen inches. Boats with motors are not allowed, so most of the fishing is done from shore. The lake trout are in shallow water early and late in the season, but go deep after the weather warms. A popular method of fishing the lake is to wade out in chest waders as far as you can, then cast heavy lures and allow them to settle as close to the bottom as possible before retrieving. Look for structure (an area affording fish food and/or shelter), where a drop off is evident, especially near a feeder stream, and you may be surprised by the results. The largest lake trout every caught in the Park was caught here (forty-three pounds). Fly fishermen do very well casting to rising fish.

Heart Lake is a hiking destination, and the pressure is not as heavy as at the more accessible lakes and streams. Landing rates reported were under one fish per hour. Most angler surveys show above average satisfaction with the over-all experience and with number and size of fish.

Heart River

A short river formed by the outlet stream at the southeast corner of Heart Lake. It flows about four miles before joining the Snake. The upper three miles are followed closely by the Heart River Trail. The river supports a population of cutthroat trout that sustains a catch rate of over one fish per hour for trout that average almost twelve inches.

Hering Lake

One of two nice backcountry cutthroat lakes near the park's south boundary. See Beula Lake for road and trail directions. To reach Hering, follow the marshy inlet on Beula's south shore.

Hering varies in size, covering up to sixty acres in years with heavy rainfall. It has a maximum depth of forty-four feet. The lake offers good fishing for cutthroat trout

Lewis Lake

The third largest lake in the park, with a very popular fishery for lake trout and browns. Lewis covers about 2700 acres, with a maximum depth of 108 feet.

The South Entrance Road follows the lake's east shore about fourteen miles from the South Entrance, between the entrance gate and West Thumb. Fishing pressure is usually heavy, thanks to easy access and to the fact that motorized boats are allowed on the lake.

The primary fisheries here are for brown trout and lake trout, with brook trout available near the tributaries, which flow in from the north and northwest. The lake's primary source is Shoshone Lake, which is drained by the Lewis-Shoshone Channel. (See Lewis River.)

Fly angling is especially popular near the main inlet and the Lewis River outlet in the spring and fall. Very large lake trout have been taken from the depths here, with deep trolling most effective for lake trout during the summer months.

Angler surveys report a landing rate of under one fish per hour, average satisfaction ratings for over-all experience, above average for size of fish caught, and below average for numbers caught. Average size of fish landed is over fifteen inches. The apparent increase in size of brown trout is encouraging.

An improved boat ramp and the Lewis Lake Campground are on the south shore. Anglers also approach the lake from the highway, where parking turn-outs are available.

Lewis River

Outlet of Shoshone Lake, inlet of Lewis Lake, with good fishing throughout the season, and trophy opportunities in the fall. The Lewis supports healthy populations of brown and brook trout, with smaller numbers of rainbow, cutthroat and lake trout.

The Lewis-Shoshone Channel, flowing 3.9 miles, is very popular during the fall, when the large brown trout from Shoshone and Lewis lakes enter to spawn. About half of angler activity in the channel occurs during this run. Angler success in catching fish averaging sixteen inches results in excellent ratings for all categories.

The segment of river between Lewis Lake and Lewis Falls offers riffle and pool fishing for smaller trout in a handsome setting throughout the summer, and for big browns in fall. From the falls to the canyon, the Lewis is a slow moving meadow stream with pan-size trout. In the canyon, the river is almost inaccessible, due to the sheer cliffs and deep canyon walls.

You can reach the channel portion of the river either by hiking the Channel Trail, located at the upper end of Lewis Lake, or by crossing Lewis Lake in a boat and then following the channel upstream. After it leaves Lewis Lake, the river is paralleled by the South Entrance Road, which provides immediate access.

The average size of fish landed for the entire river is around fourteen inches, with a landing rate under one per hour. Angler satisfaction with the experience, size of fish caught and the number of fish landed is above average. The large brown trout below Lewis Lake are more difficult to catch.

Little Robinson Creek

Tributary of Robinson Creek. See Robinson Creek for directions. Little Robinson is crossed by the West Boundary Trail immediately before its confluence with Robinson west of Bechler River Ranger Station. It offers fair fishing for brook trout that average over ten inches with landing rates under one fish per hour.

Mariposa Lake

A long hike in for rainbow and cutthroat fishing. Follow the South Boundary Trail about twenty-eight miles from the South Entrance of the park. The fish average eleven inches, with a landing rate under one fish per hour. Anglers express excellent satisfaction with the over-all experience and with number of fish caught, above average satisfaction with catch size.

Moose Creek

An inlet of Shoshone Lake, on the south shore about two miles west of Shoshone Lake Ranger Station. The Shoshone Lake Trail heading west from the ranger station provides access. Moose Creek supports populations of small brown and brook trout that average nine inches, with catch rates of just under one fish per hour.

Mountain Ash Creek

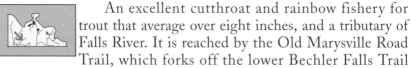

An excellent cutthroat and rainbow fishery for trout that average over eight inches, and a tributary of Falls River. It is reached by the Old Marysville Road Trail, which forks off the lower Bechler Falls Trail (skirting the east shore of Lilypad Lake). Angler surveys indicate a landing rate of nearly three fish per hour with excellent satisfaction with number and size of fish caught.

Outlet Creek

Outlet of Outlet Lake, which perches above Heart Lake about three miles east. Outlet Creek flows south to join Surprise Creek, which empties into the Heart River a quarter mile from its source at the outlet of Heart Lake. The creek is crossed by the Heart Lake Trail. Its pan-size cutthroat trout offer fair to good fishing.

Outlet Lake

A tiny lake perched above Heart Lake, offering fair fishing for small cutthroat trout. This shallow sixteen acre lake is located at an elevation of 7749 feet.

To reach it, follow the Heart Lake Trail toward the Heart River outlet at the southeast tip of the lake. Outlet Creek flows into the river from the northeast. Follow the creek to Outlet Lake.

Ouzel Creek

A tributary of the Bechler River, offering fair fishing for pan-size rainbow and cutthroat trout. Ouzel Creek empties into the Bechler at the upper end of the Bechler Meadows, a wonderful area to observe wildlife. To the north, you can see Ouzel Falls. There are no fish in the stream above the falls.

Plateau Creek

Near the junction of the Chipmunk Creek Trail and the South Boundary Trail. It has a population of cutthroat trout that average thirteen inches with landing rates over one fish per hour .

Pocket Lake

A fourteen acre off-trail lake above Shoshone Lake, with a population of cutthroat trout that provide fair fishing. To reach Pocket, follow the Pocket Creek outlet, which is crossed by the Shoshone Lake Trail. From the

DeLacy/Shoshone Trail junction, follow the Shoshone Lake Trail west to the outlet. Pocket has a maximum depth of twenty-four feet.

The lake has been involved in a cutthroat restoration project, and the previous population of brook trout has been eliminated. Recent surveys suggest this lake, at elevation 8100 feet, may be a marginal habitat to sustain a viable population of cutthroat trout. The existing trout average almost thirteen inches with reported landing rates of one fish per hour.

Polecat Creek

Accessed at Moose Falls just north of the South Entrance on the South Entrance Road. Polecat offers fair fishing for small cutthroat trout that average over seven inches in length. Landing rates of over four fish per hour have been reported.

Proposition Mountain Creek

A small tributary of Mountain Ash Creek, crossed by the Marysville Road Trail about one mile east of the Union Falls Trail junction. It offers good fishing for pan-size cutthroat and rainbow that average almost eight inches with landing rates that exceed two fish per hour.

Ranger Lake

Located near the Bechler River in the southwest corner of the park. Rainbow trout were introduced during stocking operations, but no information is available as to the present status of the fishery.

Red Creek

Tributary of the Snake, supporting pan-size cutthroat. The Heart Lake Trail follows Red Creek after fording the Snake about six miles from the South Entrance. See Heart Lake for directions.

Robinson Creek

A mountain stream offering good fishing for small brook and brown trout that average seven inches in length. Robinson is crossed by the West Boundary Trail, heading at the Bechler River Ranger Station in the far southwest corner of the Park. To reach the station, turn off Highway 47 onto Cave Falls Road, then follow the turn-off to the ranger station (Cave Falls Road dead-ends at the falls).

Robinson Creek is the first stream you cross after passing Robinson Lake and is about three miles from the ranger station.

Rock Creek

Outlet of Robinson Lake, offering some fishing for pan-size brook trout. See Robinson Lake for directions. Follow the lake's south shore to reach the outlet.

Sheridan Lake

A small, shallow lake about one mile south of Heart Lake, accessed by the Heart Lake Trail. Sheridan covers about 15 acres and is only five feet deep. It offers limited fishing for cutthroat trout.

Shoshone Creek

A small mountain stream that flows into the west end of Shoshone Lake. It can be found by hiking along the Shoshone Lake Trail approximately eight miles from the trailhead near Old Faithful. Small brown and brook trout provide good fishing, with reported catch rates of over one fish per hour.

Shoshone Lake

The largest backcountry lake in the lower forty-eight states, and second largest lake in the park. It receives little fishing pressure in comparison with more accessible lakes, but it is the most popular backcountry destination in Yellowstone. Shoshone covers about 8050 acres, with a maximum depth of 205 feet.

The lake is closed to motorized craft, but canoeing around Lewis Lake and up the Lewis-Shoshone Channel is a popular approach. Canoeists are urged to follow the Lewis Lake shoreline rather than head across the lake, in deference to precocious and powerful winds that can pick up at any time. The channel can be paddled most of the way, with a tow line or portage required for the final mile. More portaging and pulling are required in later summer and fall. Like Lewis, Shoshone has a reputation for sudden storms, so use caution in your explorations.

Trails leading into Shoshone include the Howard Eaton Trail, DeLacy Creek Trail and the Lewis-Shoshone Channel Trail. The Channel Trail heads off a primitive road just north of Lewis Lake, across the road from the Heart Lake trailhead. It is a 4 1/2 mile hike to the south end of Shoshone, where there are designated campsites. The DeLacy Creek Trail heads south from the Grand Loop Road at

DeLacy Park, between Old Faithful and West Thumb (9 1/2 miles east of Old Faithful). It is about three miles to the lake, seven to the channel. It is a longer route to the lake on the Howard Eaton Trail heading south from Old Faithful, or by way of the Bechler River Trail which begins at the South Entrance.

Once there, anglers will find that brown trout and lake trout are most prevalent, with some brook trout also available. Most of the trout caught average seventeen inches, but larger lake trout are caught at times. In the late fall the brown trout become extremely aggressive, and angler success achieves an excellent rating for those willing to chance the frequent fall storms. During the summer, if you want lake trout you will have to troll deep, but in the spring and fall they are often found in shallower water. The south shore of the lake seems more popular with successful fisherman.

Landing rates of under one fish per hour are reported by anglers, with those fishing from shore having a significantly greater landing rate than boat fishermen. Angler satisfaction with their over-all experience, size of fish caught, and number caught is above average to excellent.

Sickle Creek

Tributary of the Snake River which drains the land east of Chicken Ridge. It is reached by the Snake River Trail. Small cutthroat trout provide fair to good fishing.

Snake River

The Snake River wanders over forty miles along the south boundary of the park. It is reached only by trail except for the small section near the South Entrance. Because access requires long hikes, the Snake does not receive the fishing pressure other park waters often do.

There are several trails that follow the river, beginning with the South Boundary Trail, which heads near the South Entrance Ranger Station. To reach the headwaters, follow the trail about eleven miles from the entrance, then take the Basin Creek Trail for three miles to the Heart River Trail. Remain on the Heart River Trail for seven

miles to the Big Game Ridge Trail. Follow this trail east until you come again to the South Boundary Trail, which follows the headwaters to their source.

Cutthroat and whitefish make up the biggest share of the fish population, with some brook, lake, brown, and rainbow also available. The fish average twelve inches, with landing rates under one fish per hour. Anglers give excellent ratings for the over-all experience, for number of fish caught, and for size of fish landed. Landing rates appear to be declining when compared with previous years. This stream seems to be producing far below its fishery potential and may require special regulations to restore quality fishing.

Summit Creek

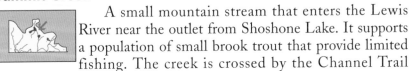

A small mountain stream that enters the Lewis River near the outlet from Shoshone Lake. It supports a population of small brook trout that provide limited fishing. The creek is crossed by the Channel Trail between Shoshone and Lewis lakes.

Surprise Creek

A tributary of Heart River, offering fair to good fishing for pan-size cutthroat trout. The creek joins the river near the Heart Lake outlet. See Heart Lake for directions.

ZONE 6

That portion of the Yellowstone River watershed that includes Yellowstone Lake, from the park's southern boundary to a point one mile downstream from the lake outlet.

lancing at a map of the park, it is Yellowstone Lake that draws the eye. Over twenty miles long and fourteen miles wide, it has an average depth of 139 feet and is 320 feet deep in places. Cupped in an ancient caldera at elevation 7733 feet, the lake is cold the year around. Even insulated waders cannot protect anglers from its chill.

Cutthroat trout, however, thrive in this environment, and the lake is home to the largest inland cutthroat population in the world. Wildlife is abundant in the vicinity of the lake, including representatives of nearly every park species.

This zone also includes the marshy wilderness beginnings of the Yellowstone River, which pours into the lake's southeast arm. Though fifty percent of the park's angling activity takes place at Yellowstone Lake, very few anglers sample the lake's remote bays or explore its myriad inlet streams.

Only thirty miles of shoreline are accessible by car, following the West Thumb-Fishing Bridge Road and the East Entrance Road. The two main trail networks within the zone are the Thorofare Trail on the lake's east shore, and Trail Creek Trail in the south. Accommodations are available at Grant Village and Lake. There are campgrounds at Grant Village, Bridge Bay, and Fishing Bridge.

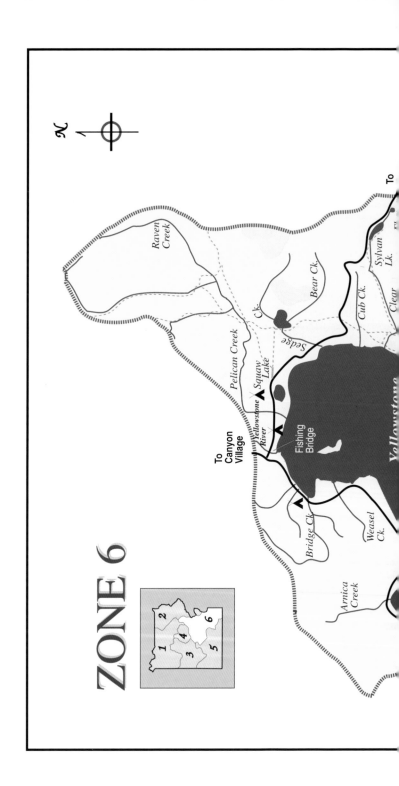

ZONE 6

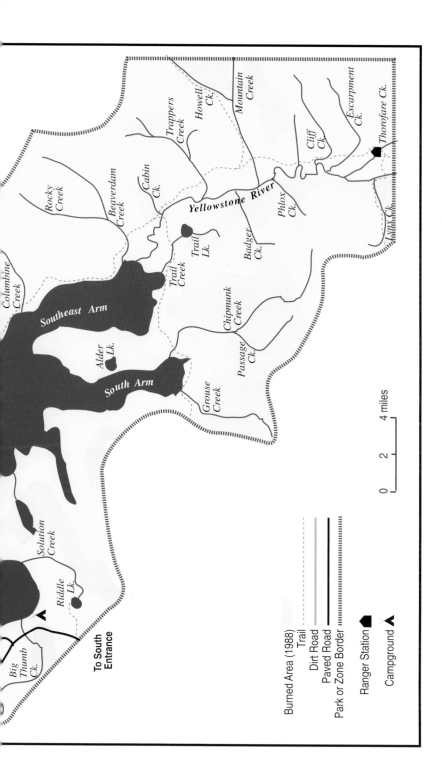

Burned Area (1988)
Trail
Dirt Road
Paved Road
Park or Zone Border

Ranger Station
Campground

0   2   4 miles

Alder Lake

A fifty-five acre lake on the west side of the promontory between the South and Southeast Arms of Yellowstone Lake. Cutthroat trout averaging ten inches offer fair fishing. Access is by boat or by bushwhack from the Trail Creek Trail. Fishing success here can be hampered by extensive algal blooms during the summer.

Arnica Creek

A small creek flowing into the north end of the West Thumb of Yellowstone Lake which is used for spawning by the lake cutthroat, but has few resident trout.

Badger Creek

A minor tributary of the Yellowstone River, flowing from the west and draining a portion of the Two Ocean Plateau. There is no convenient trail access. Badger supports a population of small cutthroat trout and is used by the lake cutthroat as spawning grounds.

Bear Creek

A small creek entering Turbid Lake from the south. It provides fair to good fishing for small cutthroat trout that average seven inches. The Bear Creek Trail, which climbs 1600 feet to Jones Pass, follows the creek much of the way. To reach the trail from the Fishing Bridge-East Entrance Road, cut off onto the service road that heads directly east at Squaw Lake. A primitive track continues around the south shore of Turbid. The Bear Creek Trail heads east (left) from the track. Reported landing rates are under one fish per hour.

Beaverdam Creek

A spawning stream for Yellowstone Lake cutthroat, entering the lake from the east near the end of the southeast arm. Rocky Creek joins Beaverdam about one mile upstream. In addition to hosting lake spawners, Beaverdam has a population of small cutthroat trout.

Beaverdam is crossed by the Thorofare Trail in a marshy meadow (the Yellowstone inlet area) about a mile beyond Monument Cairn. The mouth of Beaverdam Creek is the dead-line for motorized craft on the lake and a popular camping area. See Yellowstone River, Zone 6, for directions to the Thorofare trailhead.

Angler surveys indicate landing rates under one fish per hour, with poor satisfaction expressed with the over-all experience and number of fish.

The brush and willows of the Beaverdam area offer good camouflage for bears, and the Thorofare Trail is used by grizzlies, so be alert and make noise on the trail.

Big Thumb Creek

An inlet stream of the West Thumb of Yellowstone Lake, entering the lake just north of Grant Village. It supports a population of resident cutthroat trout and is used as spawning grounds by the lake cutthroat.

Bridge Creek

Flows south off Elephant Back Mountain, then runs east about three miles into Yellowstone Lake at Bridge Bay. It is used as spawning grounds by the lake cutthroat and supports few resident trout.

Cabin Creek

A spawning stream for Yellowstone Lake cutthroat, with its own population of small trout. The creek is crossed by the Thorofare Trail (mile 21) in the vicinity of the old Cabin Creek Patrol Cabin, which was removed after being destroyed by grizzly bears. A short trail here loops down to the Yellowstone River. See Yellowstone River, Zone 6, for directions to the trailhead.

Chipmunk Creek

Flowing west off Two Oceans Plateau into the South Arm of the lake, a spawning ground for Yellowstone Lake cutthroat.

Chipmunk is crossed by the Trail Creek Trail about a mile west of the Trail Creek Patrol Cabin. See Trail Creek for directions. A trail follows Chipmunk upstream several miles from the lake, before cutting west to follow Passage Creek.

Anglers report average satisfaction with the number of fish caught here and excellent satisfaction with the over-all experience and size of fish.

Clear Creek

A major spawning stream for Yellowstone Lake cutthroat. To reach it, follow the Thorofare trail along the east shore of Yellowstone Lake two miles to the Clear Creek Trail junction. An old horse trail also comes in here, so be sure to look for official trail markers. Thorofare crosses Clear Creek about one mile beyond the junction.

The Clear Creek Trail can be followed from Sylvan Lake to Yellowstone Lake, a descent of some 700 feet. The trailhead is at the southeast end of Sylvan immediately east of the East Entrance Road. The trail follows the creek from the lake's west shore, through a meadow below Grizzly Peak, before entering dense forest.

Landing rates of under two fish per hour have been reported, with above average angler satisfaction with over-all experiences, number of fish caught, and size. Due to bear activity, this area has a delayed opening. Check current regulations for opening date.

Cliff Creek

A small cutthroat steam, tributary of the Yellowstone River in the upper Thorofare area. It is crossed by the Thorofare Trail about two miles north of the Thorofare Ranger station. The creek is a spawning stream for Yellowstone Lake cutthroat.

Columbine Creek

A spawning stream for Yellowstone cutthroat with a resident population of small trout. It is crossed by the Thorofare Trail about three miles south of the Park Point Patrol Cabin and flows into the lake near the wrist of the Southeast Arm, about a nine mile hike from the trailhead. See Yellowstone River, Zone 6, for directions to the trailhead. The fish average almost fourteen inches with landing rates that exceed four fish per hour being reported.

Cub Creek

A spawning area for Yellowstone Lake cutthroat trout, with some smaller resident fish. Cub is crossed by the Thorofare Trail about 1 1/2 miles from the trailhead on the East Entrance Road. The Thorofare Trail follows the lake's east shore, then continues along the upper Yellowstone River.

Anglers report excellent satisfaction with their experience fishing Cub, with number of fish caught, and with size of the fish. The trout average sixteen inches with landing rates of under one fish per hour. Due to bear activity, this area has a delayed opening. Check current regulations for opening date.

Eleanor Lake

A tiny shallow lake approximately one mile east of Sylvan Lake, just off the East Entrance Road. It somehow sustains a population of cutthroat trout that provides fair fishing. Anglers report a landing rate of under one fish per hour with above average satisfaction with the experience. Angler satisfaction with number and size of fish, however, is average. These fish approach eleven inches in size.

Escarpment Creek

A tributary of the upper Yellowstone in the Thorofare area. Escarpment joins the river north of the Thorofare Ranger Station just inside the south park boundary. It is crossed by the Thorofare Trail (mile 31.5). Escarpment supports a population of small cutthroat trout and is used as a spawning area for Yellowstone Lake cutthroat.

Grouse Creek

A small stream flowing north off Chicken Ridge, emptying into the southern tip of the South Arm of Yellowstone Lake. It is crossed by the Trail Creek Trail about five miles west of the Chipmunk Creek Trail.

Small cutthroat trout are in residence here, and the stream is used as a spawning area by the lake cutthroat. Anglers report landing rates that exceed one fish per hour for trout that average thirteen inches in length.

Howell Creek

A major tributary of Mountain Creek, joining Mountain about four miles above the Mountain Creek Trail junction with the Thorofare Trail (Thorofare Trail mile 25). The Mountain Creek Trail follows Howell through Eagle Pass. Howell has a population of resident cutthroat that average seventeen inches. Landing rates of over one fish per hour are common.

Indian Pond (Squaw Lake)

A small lake about three miles east of Fishing Bridge along the East Entrance Road. It covers twenty-four acres, with a maximum depth of seventy-two feet. Fed primarily by underground springs, it provides scant spawning ground for its resident cutthroat, which are small and provide poor fishing. Past attempts at stocking the pond did not improve the fishing and were discontinued. Yellowstone Lake cutthroat probably enter the pond during high water.

Lynx Creek

A minor tributary of the Yellowstone River, flowing from the west and draining the southern portion of the Two Ocean Plateau. The South Boundary Trail follows Lynx Creek for several miles before the confluence.

Lynx supports a population of small cutthroat trout and is used by Yellowstone Lake cutthroat as spawning grounds.

Meadow Creek

A tiny stream that flows into Yellowstone Lake near the Park Point Patrol Cabin on the Thorofare Trail. It has a resident population of small cutthroat and is a spawning area for the lake cutthroat. Resident trout average over nine inches in length with landing rates under one fish per hour.

Mountain Creek

A tributary of the upper Yellowstone in the Thorofare area, which serves as a spawning stream for Yellowstone Lake cutthroat. It is crossed by the Thorofare Trail (mile 26) and accessed by the Mountain Creek Trail, which heads northeast from Thorofare at mile 25. The Mountain Creek Trail follows Mountain Creek for about four miles before following Howell Creek north toward Eagle Pass.

In addition to the lake spawners, Mountain Creek supports a population of small resident cutthroat. For more information abut the Thorofare Trail, see Yellowstone River, Zone 6. The trout average over thirteen inches with landing rates that exceed one fish per hour.

Passage Creek

A tributary of Chipmunk Creek, which flows into Yellowstone Lake's south arm, primarily a spawning season fishery. See Chipmunk Creek for directions.

Anglers report average satisfaction with number of fish caught and excellent satisfaction with the over-all experience and size of fish.

Pelican Creek

A major spawning area for Yellowstone Lake cutthroat. Pelican offers good to excellent fishing for trout averaging fourteen inches.

Access to the stream is by a foot trail that begins east of Fishing Bridge across the road from Squaw Lake. The first two miles of the stream are closed to fishing, so plan accordingly if you follow the stream rather than take the trail. The Pelican Creek Trail hits the creek about six miles upstream, a three mile hike. Following the creek through the Pelican Valley, be aware that this is grizzly country. Keep alert and make noise on the trail.

Angler surveys indicate a landing rate of fourteen-inch fish over one fish per hour. Anglers rate the over-all fishing experience, number of fish caught and size of fish caught as excellent.

Phlox Creek

A minor tributary of the Yellowstone River, flowing from the west and draining a portion of the Two Ocean Plateau. There is no convenient trail access. Phlox supports a population of small cutthroat trout and is used as spawning grounds by Yellowstone Lake trout.

Raven Creek

A small tributary of Pelican Creek offering good fishing for cutthroat trout that average almost seventeen inches in length. To fish the stream, follow the Pelican Creek Trail about seven miles to the Pelican Springs Patrol Cabin. See Pelican Creek for directions. Head west (left) at the trail junction. This trail crosses Raven in one mile, then continues on to a junction with the Pelican Cone Trail, and an old service road that comes out near Turbid Lake east of Fishing Bridge. (Turbid Lake is acidic and holds no fish.) Landing rates often exceed three fish per hour. In spite of low landing rates, Raven Creek is given excellent satisfaction responses for over-all experience, number of fish, and size of fish caught.

Riddle Lake

An easily accessed hike-in lake east of the South Entrance Road a little more than two miles south of Grant Campground. Intense fishing pressure decimated the lake's native cutthroat population, leading to a complete closure for two years. The lake is now open for catch-and-release fishing only for trout that average thirteen inches in length. Landing rates are below one fish per hour.

Hikers should be aware that the Riddle Lake Trail is frequented by grizzly bears. Hike in groups of four or more, and make plenty of noise on the trail.

Rocky Creek

A tributary of Beaverdam Creek, joining Beaverdam about one mile upstream from Beaverdam's entrance into Yellowstone Lake. Like Beaverdam, Rocky serves as a spawning stream for Yellowstone Lake cutthroat and maintains a population of small resident cutthroat. See Beaverdam Creek and Yellowstone River, Zone 6, for complete trail directions.

Sedge Creek

A small creek that flows into Turbid Lake from the northeast, offering fair to good fishing for small cutthroat trout. Sedge also drains Turbid into Yellowstone Lake near Butte Springs Picnic Area. Turbid is a highly acidic geothermal lake that supports no fish.

Sedge Creek receives below average angler satisfaction responses for number of fish caught and over-all experience. Average satisfaction was reported for size of fish.

Solution Creek

The outlet of Riddle Lake, flowing about ten miles into the West Thumb of Yellowstone Lake.

To reach the upper creek, follow the Riddle Lake Trail which heads east from the South Entrance Road a little more than four miles south of Grant Campground. It is a two mile hike to the lake. Solution drains out on the lake's east shore. The upper creek supports a population of small cutthroat.

The lower creek, inlet to Yellowstone Lake, can be reached by a three mile boat trip across West Thumb. The inlet is fished for spawning lake cutthroat.

Squaw Lake (See Indian Pond.)

Sylvan Lake

A narrow lake, nestled in dense forest, adjacent to the East Entrance Road just east of Sylvan Pass. It offers fair fishing for cutthroat trout averaging twelve inches.

Because of its accessibility from the road (there is a picnic area on the northwest shore), it has received heavy angling pressure. A decline in fish population lead to the imposition of a catch-and-release restriction here. Size of catch and landing rate have subsequently increased.

SYLVAN LAKE

There are two inlet streams, one entering from the northeast, the other from southeast. The outlet drains west into Clear Creek.

Anglers indicate average satisfaction with their over-all experience at Sylvan and with the number of fish caught, and above average satisfaction with size. The current landing rate is under one fish per hour.

Thorofare Creek

The highest tributary of the Yellowstone within the park. The Thorofare Trail crosses the creek in the vicinity of Thorofare Ranger Station, where a ranger is usually in residence throughout the summer.

MULES EAR

Thorofare's cutthroat trout provide excellent fishing for those willing to make the hike. Anglers report excellent satisfaction with the experience and the number of fish caught. Landing rates approaching six fish per hour have been reported for trout averaging over eighteen inches in length.

Trail Creek

Inlet and outlet of Trail Lake, flowing about two miles from the lake into the southern tip of the Southeast Arm of Yellowstone Lake. Trail Creek Trail crosses the creek a mile before fording the Yellowstone River and joining the Thorofare Trail.

Trail Creek is a major access into the southern Yellowstone Lake area. It begins at Heart lake Patrol Cabin, reached by way of the Heart Lake Trail that heads on the South Entrance Road across from Lewis Lake.

Trail creek supports a resident population of small cutthroat trout and is used as a spawning area for Yellowstone Lake trout.

Trail Lake

A shallow wilderness lake covering fifty-five acres, about one mile southeast of the southern tip of the Southeast Arm of Yellowstone Lake. Trail Creek Trail crosses Trail Lake's outlet stream (Trail Creek) a little more than two miles east of Trail Creek Patrol Cabin. Follow the creek to Trail Lake. Anglers who have visited the lake give it an excellent rating for over-all experience and fishing quality. The trout average over seventeen inches in length with landing rates under one fish per hour.

Trappers Creek

A spawning stream for Yellowstone Lake cut-throat, with its own population of small trout. Trapper is about two miles south of Cabin Creek, crossed by the Thorofare Trail (mile 23). See Yellowstone River, Zone 6, for directions to the trailhead.

Weasel Creek

A small creek flowing into Yellowstone Lake about a mile and a half south of Natural Bridge. It is used for spawning by the lake cutthroat during high water years when the water levels flood the road culvert.

Yellowstone Lake

The central feature of Yellowstone National Park, remnant of an enormous volcanic caldera, covering about 87,450 acres, with an average depth of 139 feet, maximum depth 320 feet.

Visitors can anticipate almost daily late morning winds out of the southwest, with waves whipped up to five or six feet. Boaters who swamp risk death from rapid hypothermia in the lake's chilly waters. Don't take chances—this lake has claimed many victims over the years.

Though a variety of fish species have been introduced to the lake at one time or another, the only surviving gamefish (other than some successful baitfish) are cutthroat trout. Yellowstone Lake supports the largest population of cutthroat trout in the world. The lake is currently managed with the primary objective of providing harvestable cutthroat for the park's wildlife—the bears, mink and waterfowl.

The Yellowstone River is its major inlet, entering from the southeast and flowing out at the north. In addition, there are over 124 smaller tributaries. The lake is in a beautiful setting, with the Absaroka Range to the east and other handsome peaks and plateaus gracing every vista. A fine view of the lake and its environment is available at the Lake Butte Overlook just off the East Entrance Road

All roads into the park eventually lead to Yellowstone Lake, but only thirty miles of the shoreline are accessible to motor vehicles. The remaining eighty miles of shoreline can only be reached by boat, foot, or horseback. The two primary trails that explore the shoreline and tributaries are the Thorofare Trail, following the lake's east shore, and the Trail Creek Trail, which accesses the south and southeast arms.

YELLOWSTONE LAKE HOTEL

The most popular route to this trail is by way of the Heart Lake Trail, which begins on the east side of the South Entrance Road just north of Lewis Lake. Few park visitors take advantage of these trails, which offer a true wilderness experience and access to the spawning streams of the lake's big cutthroat.

The average size of Yellowstone Lake cutthroat is over fifteen inches, with some over twenty inches landed. Fishing here is primarily a catch-and-release proposition, since regulations restrict keeping to two fish under 13 inches, and there are comparatively few fish in Yellowstone under 13 inches caught! You'll hear few complaints, however, since these regulations are directly responsible for restoring the lake's original state of bounty after decades of depletion.

Yellowstone is fished from both boat and shore. Many shore anglers use dry flies to tempt the surface feeders found close to

YELLOWSTONE LAKE FROM NORTH SHORE

sand bars, rocky points, and at spring and creek inlets. A favorite shore fishing area is close to Bridge Bay Campground, where a sand bar and shallow water provide a natural cruising ground for hungry cutthroat. Most of the time, if the light is right and the air is calm, you can see the direction the fish are moving. A well-placed cast ahead of the fish can bring the slow, slurping strike of feeding trout.

But the advantage belongs to boating anglers, according to catch reports. There are public boat launches on the north and west shores, including a full service marina at Bridge Bay, and a boat ramp at Grant Village. Rental boats and guides are available at the marina, as are canoe tows and ferries across the lake. Boaters must secure a Boat Permit. Anglers piloting their own craft should be wary of sudden severe weather changes and would be well advised to always stay within easy reach of shore. Be cautious near shore also since rocky areas can extend into the lake, causing obstructions to safe boating. Acquire the necessary information concerning the lake prior to departure. Be sure to read the boating regulations carefully, since portions of the lake are off limits to motorized craft.

Yellowstone Lake receives between thirty and forty per cent of the park's angler use. The northwest portion of the lake is most heavily fished, and the central and southern portions least fished.

The more remote areas of the lake provide a higher success rate and larger catch size. The average landing rate for the entire lake is around one fish per hour. The most recent angler survey report shows excellent satisfaction with the over-all experience and size of fish landed, and above average satisfaction with number of fish caught. Boaters in the remote areas need to remember that the arms of the lake have special restrictions, including five mph speed limits and no-power areas. Also, boats over sixteen feet in length in the five mph speed zones can come no closer than 1/4 mile of the shoreline.

Yellowstone River

The wilderness section of the Yellowstone River, between the lake and the south boundary of the park. The area through which it flows is known as The Thorofare.

One popular access to the Thorofare is to hitch a ride on a boat to the Southeast Arm of Yellowstone Lake (charters are available), then join the Thorofare Trail to hike upriver. You can also hike into the area on the Thorofare Trail, which heads south from the East Entrance Road about a mile east of Yellowstone Lake. It is a twenty mile walk to the little loop trail that first leads down to Yellowstone River in the vicinity of the old Cabin Creek Patrol Cabin (removed after being destroyed by grizzly bears), and about thirty-one miles to Thorofare Ranger Station, just inside the south boundary of the park.

This is an incredibly scenic area, including the beautiful Yellowstone itself, as well as the huge meadows through which it winds, the impressive Two Ocean Plateau to the west, and the Three Trident escarpments to the east.

Angler survey results for this portion of the river are of questionable reliability due to the small sample size, but of those received, satisfaction ratings are excellent for both number and size of fish caught (averaging sixteen inches). The number of available fish decreases rapidly after the spawning run, which is usually over by August.

THE GRAND TETONS SEEN FROM HENRYS FORK OF THE SNAKE RIVER

The Greater Yellowstone Area

Outstanding waters beyond Yellowstone Park boundaries.

The boundaries of Yellowstone National Park were drawn to encompass the area's many natural wonders, but broad as they are, they fail to capture all the magnificent fishing waters that are found in this piece of salmonid heaven. The following supplement briefly describes many of the more popular waters located outside park boundaries, but still within the "Greater Yellowstone Area." Consider these waters if the park crowds become too burdensome or the park weather too miserable. These waters may also provide fishing and camping opportunities for your inbound and outbound journeys.

The author has selected those fisheries that lie within reasonable driving distance from one of the park entrances. He is acutely aware that there are definite gender and regional differences with regard to defining "reasonable driving distances," and cautions the reader that where fanaticism is an issue, the term could mean almost anything. Since the author grew up in the open spaces of west, be prepared for some stretching of the word "reasonable."

The park entrances will serve in this section as the starting point for purposes of trip planning. A state license is required to fish in any of the waters outside the boundaries of Yellowstone National Park.

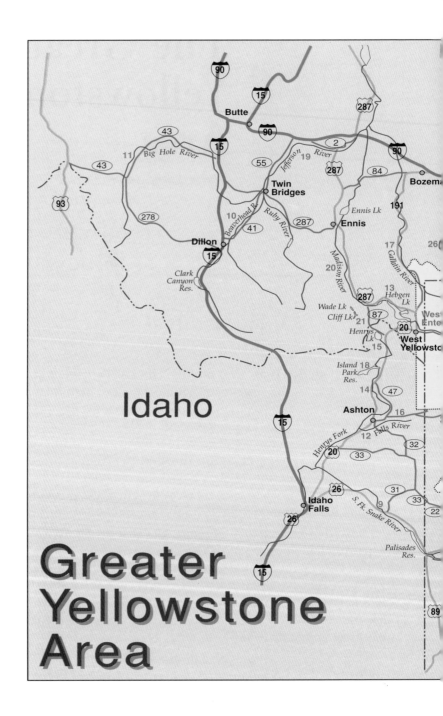

Greater
Yellowstone
Area

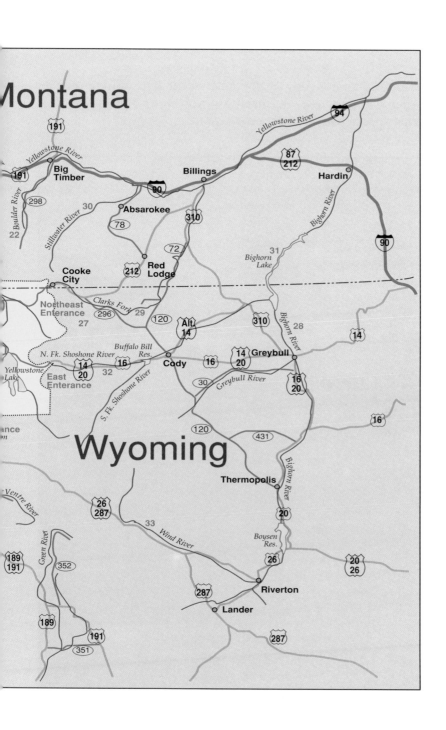

Be certain to obtain a copy of the most recent state fishing regulations when you purchase your license so you won't be surprised if a stream has special regulations for management purposes.

THE SNAKE RIVER ORIGINATES IN GLORIOUS SURROUNDINGS

South Entrance Fisheries

Flat Creek (1)

Flat Creek is Wyoming's single "fly fishing only" stream. Located by Jackson (the section that flows through town is restricted to children 13 years of age and younger), the reach most interesting to fly anglers flows through the National Elk Refuge. This area has special restrictions, so check the regulations regarding opening dates. This is not an easy stream to fish, as the cutthroat trout are wary, well-educated, and sometimes large. Check with local tackle shops for current hatches and successful flies.

Grassy Lake Reservoir and Lake of the Woods (2)

The Grassy Lake Road (Ashton Reclamation Road) is found just north of Flagg Ranch, about 2 miles from the Yellowstone National Park south entrance. Follow this dirt and gravel road for 9 miles and you will reach Grassy Lake Reservoir, which holds a good population of lake trout and cutthroat trout. Float tubes are often used here and motorized boats are allowed.

If all is quiet at Grassy Lake, continue past Grassy Lake to the Camp Loll turn off. Follow the Camp Loll road to the Boy Scout camp, which is located on Lake of the Woods. There are some nice rainbow trout here waiting for the right angler to discover their feeding patterns.

Grey's River and Nearby Waters (3)

Cutthroat trout predominate in the Grey's River, with some brown trout and whitefish also available. Access to Grey's River begins just south of Alpine Junction, near the backwaters of Palisades Reservoir. Alpine Junction is reached by following US 26 (and the Snake River) south from Jackson about 35 miles. At Alpine Junction, turn south on US 89 and cross the Snake. The Grey's River Road joins US 89 a half mile south of the bridge, and parallels the river its entire length. Several forest service campgrounds are found along the river.

The Little Grey's River is a popular tributary and contains smaller cutthroat trout. If you are interested in a more challenging experience, try the small lakes located on the tributaries, like the

Murphy Lakes, Lake Barstow, the Crow Creek Lakes and the sleeper—Corral Creek Lake (Large shrimp-fed cutthroat trout are reported by fishing fanatics with sore feet).

Gros Ventre River and Nearby Lakes (4)
Nine miles north of Jackson, US 26/89 crosses the Gros Ventre River. Access to the river is found from the Gros Ventre Road which follows the river almost to its head. The river receives less angling pressure than the Snake and contains cutthroat trout, rainbow trout and whitefish.

Located along the river are Lower Slide Lake and Upper Slide Lake, both of which contain trout and whitefish. If you're looking for rainbow trout, the pocket water below Lower Slide Lake is a good location. July and August are usually the better months to fish the Gros Ventre.

Hoback River (5)
The Hoback River joins the Snake thirteen miles south of Jackson by US 26/89, at Hoback Junction. Anglers can follow the river via Highway 187 for fifteen miles through Hoback Canyon. The best fishing for the Hoback's medium-sized trout cutthroat trout comes during the stonefly hatch, generally the first week in July. The river also has a healthy contains a whitefish population.

Jackson Lake (6)
This is a deep, cold, glacial lake that holds cutthroat and brown trout and trophy-sized lake trout. The state record lake trout, weighing 50 pounds, was taken in Jackson Lake.

Excellent fishing begins right after ice out, usually in mid-May, and continues until the surface water warms and the fish seek deeper structure. In mid-September, the surface waters again cool and the fish move into accessible, shallower water. Local marinas have boats and guides available or can provide information on the more productive spots for bank anglers.

Smaller Lakes of Grand Teton National Park (7)
Leigh Lake, Jenny Lake, Bradley Lake, Taggert Lake and Phelps Lake offer a variety of fishing experiences depending on how adven-

turous (i.e., how far you want to walk) the angler is. These lakes offer abundant brook and cutthroat trout. Leigh, Jenny and Phelps also harbor lake trout. The *Grand Teton National Park Guide* will show you the locations of trail heads and access points.

Snake River (8)

After leaving Yellowstone Park, the Snake flows towards Jackson Lake and the Jackson Hole Valley. Access to the river is not a problem since most of the river flows through public lands. The size of the river is imposing and floating is the more effective method of fishing, especially below Jackson Dam. There are areas where the river is braided with many channels, so an angler not floating can successfully bank fish. Heavy run-off in late May, June and July impedes fishing in the main river, so lakes may offer a better experience until the run-off clears.

The Snake River cutthroat trout is the dominant fish in the river along with numerous whitefish and smaller numbers of brown and brook trout. Cutthroat trout readily take dry flies, making the Snake a great river for beginning fly anglers to experience success.

After the Snake River leaves the Jackson Hole Valley, it flows south and west through the Snake River Canyon and eventually reaches Palisades Reservoir in Idaho. US 26 follows the river for most of this distance. Throughout the Snake River Canyon there are numerous access points for bank anglers. Keep in mind that the water has heavy currents and a slick bottom. Inquire at the local tackle shops about current hatches and successful angling techniques.

South Fork of the Snake River (9)

The Snake River is known as the South Fork as it emerges below Palisades Dam. Highway 26 from Alpine Junction borders the east shore of Palisades Reservoir and provides access to the river below the dam for several miles. The South Fork is noted as a blue ribbon fishery because of its fertile water and rapid fish growth. Huge brown trout are found in the South Fork, where an unofficial Idaho state record brown trout 35 pounds was landed. Four and five pound fish are relatively common. Besides the brown trout, cutthroat trout, rainbow trout, whitefish and an occasional lake trout are available. This is a big river and it is from boat or raft that one can best fish its runs and channels.

Roads parallel much of the riverbank, so bank anglers are able to sample the fishing. From June through October the South Fork receives more sustained fishing pressure than any other Eastern Idaho stream. The South Fork salmon fly hatch generally starts around the beginning of July at the river's mouth and proceeds upstream four to five miles per day. This hatch produces a feeding activity that is a fly fisherman's dream, as large fish become unwary and come to any lure or fly resembling the current table fare.

Both drift and powerboat outfitters are available in the surrounding towns, and local tackle shops can provide information and guides. The canyon section below Conant Valley includes 27 miles of beautiful scenery and wild trout. Here there are no paralleling roads, but an excellent hiking trail follows the east bank and anglers can walk in or boat down for outstanding cutthroat trout and brown trout fishing.

JENNY LAKE IN GRAND TETON NATIONAL PARK

WEST ENTRANCE FISHERIES

Beaverhead River (10)

Follow Highway 287 about two hours northwest from West Yellowstone, through Ennis, Montana to Twin Bridges, Montana. Montana Highway 41 follows the Beaverhead River south, upstream, to Dillon, Montana. Interstate 15 follows the river an additional 22 miles upstream, to Clark Canyon Reservoir. The Beaverhead is known as a big fish river, especially the upper section from Clark Canyon Reservoir downstream to the Barrett Diversion Dam, south of Dillion. Heavy streamside cover makes the river difficult to access for the wading angler. Also, most land along the entire river is private, so permission is required before crossing to reach the water.

The upper Beaverhead supports tremendous trout growth rates and populations of over 2000 trout per mile. Fishing is difficult because of brushy banks, swift current, narrow channels and thick willows. Float fishing is the preferred method of angling. The stretch from Barrett's to Dillon provides the best opportunity for bank fishing, as the river slows and flows through meadows. Brown trout dominate the fishery, with rainbow trout a distant second.

The lower Beaverhead from Barrett Dam to Anderson Lane receives light fishing pressure but still contains high densities of trout. It is often said that if anglers can catch fish on the Beaverhead, they can catch them anywhere! Each year fish weighing over ten pounds are reported caught from this river.

Big Hole River (11)

Twin Bridges, Montana, two hours northwest from West Yellowstone, lies just south of the confluence of the Big Hole River, and the Beaverhead River. These two rivers, along with the Ruby River, merge and form the north-flowing Jefferson River. The Big Hole is a nationally recognized blue ribbon trout stream. It is also home to the last significant stream-residing population of grayling outside of Alaska and Canada. Even though it is a small river, the Big Hole receives tremendous fishing pressure, especially during the salmon fly hatch in early summer.

Brook trout dominate the headwater section of the Big Hole until Ralston, then rainbow trout appear to dominate to Melrose. From Melrose to the mouth, the habitat favors the brown trout. The Big Hole supports a trophy fish population and the potential exists for an angler to catch big fish. Fly anglers appear to do better on this river than spin or bait anglers.

From Twin Bridges one can follow the river upstream by following the road to Glen. From Glen, Interstate 15 generally follows the river north, through and beyond Melrose. About 8 miles north of Melrose, state highway 43 follows the river west and south for over 40 miles. Access for both floating and wading is found either from road bridges or developed access areas. Much of the river flows through private land, so be certain to ask permission before crossing private property.

Falls River (12)

Often overlooked because of its nearness to the Henry's Fork of the Snake River, Falls River offers a rainbow-cutthroat fishery whose potential has not been fully realized. There are good populations of rainbow trout that do not experience the pressure found on the Henry's Fork. The Falls River crosses US highway 20 about 60 miles southeast of West Yellowstone, between the Idaho towns of Ashton and St. Anthony. Access to the upper river is found by following the Ashton-Flagg Ranch Reclamation Road or the Cave Falls Road north of Ashton. Runoff is a problem in the early season, so it's best to fish after June.

Hebgen Lake (13)

With the end of its southern arm located just a few miles north of West Yellowstone, Hebgen Lake receives heavy recreational use. Even so, this lake has great fishing potential. Brown trout, rainbow trout and whitefish provide the sport fishing activity.

Float tubers are discovering the surface feeding "gulpers" in the Madison Arm and the mouth of the South Fork. Bank anglers catch large, hungry brown trout just after ice out (May and early June) by walking the shoreline and casting large spoons and spinners. Trolling for rainbows and browns is the most productive summer technique,

RAILROAD RANCH (HARRIMAN STATE PARK) ON HENRY'S FORK

although arm chair bait fishing from the bank is certainly popular. Highways 287 and 191 border the north and south shores of the lake, and a forest road follows the western shore, so finding fishable areas is not a problem. There are also several boat ramps within easy driving distance from West Yellowstone.

Henry's Fork (14)

The Henry's Fork of the Snake River heads in the outflow of Henry's Lake, less than half an hours drive southwest of West Yellowstone. Arguably one of the finest trout streams in the west, this blue ribbon rainbow trout fishery extends over 120 miles until it joins with the South Fork of the Snake to form the main Snake River near Rexburg, Idaho. The ten miles of the river between Island Park Dam and Osborne Bridge on Highway 191 is probably the most famous stretch, and includes both the "Box Canyon" and the "Railroad Ranch".

HENRY'S LAKE

Large rainbows, some over 20 pounds, are often reported from the three miles of nutrient rich waters flowing through the Box. Hooking the large trout and landing it are two different experiences and few of the larger fish are ever brought to the net. The river widens and becomes slower as it leaves the Box Canyon, and roadside access is easy. The next few miles downstream is probably the most heavily fished section of the river. The "Railroad Ranch" (Harriman State Park) provides nearly perfect dry fly fishing conditions.

Below Osborne Bridge the river is not as easily approached and the angler is advised to get instructions from the tackle shops in Last Chance on access points, especially if you are thinking of floating the lower stretches of river. There are several large waterfalls you must avoid, so be very cautious. The Henry's Fork does not have the run-off problems many of the Greater Yellowstone streams encounter, so it is a "best bet" for early season fishing. The river between St. Anthony and Ashton is often overlooked and may offer excellent fishing for the less experienced angler. The lower river also has a population of brown trout that are becoming more evident in reported landing rates.

Henry's Lake (15)

Located 18 miles southwest West Yellowstone via US 20 is Henry's Lake, the trophy fishing lake often called the "best trout pond in the west." The lake contains cutthroat, cutthroat-rainbow hybrid and brook trout. Hybrids commonly reach the nine pound range and brook trout are caught that exceed five pounds.

Trolling and float tube fishing are the most effective methods since bank fishing is limited by the shallow shoreline. Bank anglers find most success off the cliffs on the south side of the lake and on the north side by the Fish Hatchery or Wild Rose Marina.

Fishing in the early morning or late evening brings the best success. Almost daily, winds whip the waters from mid-morning until early evening, so plan accordingly. Henry's is a shallow lake and as the water warms in July and August weeds grow up to near the surface. Under these conditions the fish congregate at the mouths of streams and springs. Float tube fishing and fly fishing from anchored boats becomes the best technique for reaching the big trout during this period. Experts predict a state record brook trout will soon be caught from this outstanding fishery. Check with the local tackle shops for current fishing information.

Horseshoe Lake (16)

This lake is included because it has one of the few grayling populations available to the angler. The Idaho Department of Fish and Game is trying to sustain a grayling fishery in this lake and has had some success. It is reached by taking the Cave Falls Road, which intersects US 20 north of Ashton, Idaho to the Horseshoe Lake Road turnoff. Float tubing is the best technique to reach these alpine fish.

Gallatin River (17)

The Gallatin River leaves Yellowstone Park and begins its long flow north to where it joins the Madison and Jefferson to form the Missouri. Highway 191 follows the river north from West Yellowstone towards Bozeman for approximately 30 miles. The uppermost section of the Gallatin is mostly a series of riffles and can be effectively waded and fished. Beginning fly anglers do well in this area because of open channels and a large number of willing rainbows and whitefish.

A series of tributaries, most notably the West Fork, continue to add water to the Gallatin and it takes on the features of a larger river, with runs, pools and large rapids for the remainder of the canyon section. As the Gallatin leaves the canyon section, the most productive reach occurs and continues beyond the Shedd's Bridge near Gallatin Gateway. Rainbow and brown trout inhabit this stretch and fish in the ten pound class are sometimes caught. Floating is not permitted in the upper Gallatin, but is allowed below the East Gallatin confluence. Below this point the river is best fished by floating.

Island Park Reservoir (18)

Island Park Reservoir is a shallow, dammed section of the Henry's Fork of the Snake, located just upstream from the famed Box Canyon stretch. Recently this reservoir was chemically treated to remove trash fish and restocked with rainbow trout. These fish have the potential to reach large size in the coming years. The west end of the reservoir and the south shoreline bays, known as "The Fingers," are favorite locations. Float tubing is becoming more popular, but trolling is still the most consistently used and productive technique. Bank anglers report success by the dam and also at the West End Campground.

Jefferson River (19)

The north-flowing Jefferson River begins just south of Twin Bridges, Montana, two hours northwest from West Yellowstone, at the confluence of the Big Hole River, the Beaverhead River, and the Ruby River, all fine trout streams in themselves. The Jefferson is one of the underrated rivers in southwestern Montana. A headwater of the Missouri, it flows about seventy miles from its origin to its confluence with the Madison and Gallatin Rivers.

The Jefferson has a gradual gradient and slowly meanders throughout its course. Drought conditions and irrigation withdrawals impact the fragile fishery and inhibit its productivity. In spite of these problems, the Jefferson has good fishing for brown and rainbow trout. The most popular reach, between Twin Bridges and Cardwell, has the best water conditions and habitat. This is the area where most guided float fishing trips are planned. It is best fished in the spring and fall before the river warms and the irrigation season begins.

Spin anglers have good success on this stream and often outfish fly anglers. Bank anglers have to walk to reach the best water, whereas floating increases your options. Wading can be difficult because of deep water and steep banks. In spite of these difficulties, the Jefferson is a river where you can usually catch some fish.

Madison River (20)

The upper Madison, beginning where the river leaves Hebgen Lake, is probably the most famous of Montana's trout streams. It is also the most heavily used fishery in the state and annually becomes even more popular. U.S. Highway 287 parallels the river from Hebgen Lake to Ennis, Montana. This 50 miles of river is often described as being a "fifty mile riffle".

Special regulations have been implemented to produce a "large, wild trout fishery." Recent electroshocking census data on the upper Madison showed fish populations in excess of 3000 trout per mile, with rainbows being more prevalent. Brown trout and whitefish are also numerous. The lower Madison, below Ennis Lake, is heavily influenced by higher water temperatures, and the summer months do not produce good angler success.

The salmon fly hatch in late June and July brings anglers from across the nation intent on finding the "Head of the Hatch" and the gluttonous feeding that it inspires on all trout. However, many experts feel that the best fishing comes later in the season, when even beginning anglers experience productive days and high numbers of fish landed. The river is wadeable but caution is advised, as the volume of water can vary and the bottom is slippery. Floating, of course, provides greater access, and there are many outfitters ready to assist the interested angler.

Wade and Cliff Lakes (21)
This pair of long, narrow lakes, lying north of Henry's Lake and west of Hebgen Lake, are best fished early in the season. Both lakes hold rainbow trout; trophy brown trout have been caught in Wade Lake. The lakes are reached by turning southwest onto a secondary road from US 287, one mile west of its junction with Montana 87.

NORTH ENTRANCE FISHERIES

Boulder River (22)

The Boulder River, a riffle and boulder-pocket water type stream, heads on the northwest flank of the Beartooth Mountains and flows north about 40 miles to join the Yellowstone River at the town of Big Timber, Montana. Big Timber is located on Interstate 90 about 30 miles east of Livingston, Montana, which lies 53 miles north of the north park entrance via US 89. Most of the river is followed by road, but the lower section runs through private land and access is limited. Brown trout and rainbow trout are found in the lower section.

The upper section, within the Gallatin National Forest and above the falls, has great fishing for rainbows and easy access. Fishing pressure is greatest in July and August. The secret to successfully fishing the Boulder is to fish the pocket water and swifter sections.

Shields River (23)

The Shields River flows south into the Yellowstone River about 4 miles east of Livingston, Montana, about a half mile east of the US 89 highway bridge over the Yellowstone. US 89 and county roads follow it for most of its length.

Electrofishing surveys of this stream indicate good populations of brown trout in the two pound range. The headwaters offer rainbow trout, brookies and cutthroat in plentiful numbers. Fishing pressure is light and best fishing occurs in the early season or fall.

Spring Creeks (24)

Most of the quality spring creeks are privately owned and require reservations and rod fees. The best way to find out about fishing on the spring creeks around Livingston, Montana is to call the Livingston fly shops, where they may be able to book you a spot. Bookings in mid-summer can be hard to come by. The creeks lie about 8 miles south of Livingston. Nelson's Spring Creek parallels the Yellowstone River on its east side, and Armstrong and DePuys (two named stretches of the same water) Spring Creek parallels the Yellowstone River to the west.

Rainbows are the dominant fish with many in the two to five pound class. Because these creeks are spring fed, the water temperature remains an almost constant 55° F., and fishing can be quite good as early as March. Fly fishing only is required and the fishing is challenging. The best dry fly action is from mid-June thru mid-August.

Private Lakes (25)

Lenz, Chase and Story are private lakes with large trout, some in the ten pound range, that are located in the Yellowstone River valley between the north park entrance and Livingston, Montana.

Rod fees and reservations are required. Check with local tackle shops concerning location and reservations.

Yellowstone River (26)

The 60 miles of the Yellowstone River from Gardiner to Livingston provides an opportunity for an angler to catch browns, rainbows and cutthroats. This section of the Yellowstone usually is better for fly anglers in mid-July, after the run-off clears. Bait and spin anglers do well in the spring.

This is a big river, so avoid fishing the middle of the river in the slow straight runs and instead concentrate on the margins and eddies. The edges of riffles, bends in the river, undercut banks, boulders, lower ends of islands, riprapped banks and other structure should be your target areas. Concentrate on these productive areas and you will improve your results.

The Middle Yellowstone from Livingston to Columbus is an under utilized fishery even though water quality and trout numbers remain high. If you don't have much time, you would be wise to let a qualified guide float you through a section of the river and teach you how to successfully approach the Yellowstone. There are numerous access points for both floaters, waders and bank anglers all along the river.

NORTHEAST ENTRANCE FISHERIES

Absaroka Beartooth Wilderness (27)
Lying southeast of the park entrance, this large wilderness area contains numerous streams and over 435 lakes holding fish. The Beartooth Fishing Guide by Pat Marcuson details this area and makes an excellent reference. The Forest Service also has special regulations for the wilderness area, so check at Gardiner, Big Timber or Red Lodge for more information.

Bighorn River (28)
The angler intent on stretching the definition of "reasonable distance from Yellowstone National Park" must sample this fishing before leaving the area. Almost every western fishing guide book, fishing newsletter and outdoor magazine features an article concerning the Bighorn River. The Bighorn River is reached by takeing US 212 northeast from the park entrance to Interstate 90 eleven miles east of Billings, Montana. Take the Interstate east to Hardin, Montana. At Hardin, turn south on Highway 313 to Fort Smith. We won't distract you with mileages; this is for serious fishing.

    The river after it leaves the Bighorn Lake (a reservoir) is a tailwater fishery. The thirteen miles of river below the dam have the features of a big spring creek, including rich and abundant food sources. Trout populations are unbelievably high, with over 4000 brown and 1000 rainbows per mile estimated from recent electroshocking surveys. The number of fish over thirteen inches per mile doubles or triples the number found in other Montana blue ribbon fisheries.

    With fish numbers like this it is no wonder that a crowd of anglers are found working most of the water. If you are interested in solitude, pick another area, since boats pack the river during the peak summer months. Resident anglers prefer the river in the spring and fall, when the congestion is not as evident.

    Access to the river is limited. Prime water is located within the Crow Indian Reservation and public access is almost exclusive to the specific sites provided by the Montana Department of Fish and Wildlife and Parks or National Park Service land. Float fishing is

preferred, since there are few areas where anglers can wade across the river and the current runs heavy. An angler can, however, hike up and down the river from the access sites, staying within the high water mark, and find prime fishing spots.

Fly anglers, spin casters and bait anglers all report successful experiences. Tackle restrictions do exist, so check the regulations. Local tackle shops will arrange guide service, rent boats and even do a shuttle service if needed. The Bighorn, as with all blue ribbon fisheries, can disappoint any fisherman. The angler who adapts to the prevailing conditions, asks questions about techniques and methods, and observes local anglers' strategies seldom gets "skunked" on any river.

Clark's Fork (29)
The upper meadow area of the Clark's Fork parallels US 212 and then WY 296 after leaving Cooke City, MT, a town just outside the northeast park entrance. This southeast trending section and its tributaries are popular with local anglers and offer good fishing for brooks, rainbows and cutthroat trout. Beyond Sunlight Ck. campground the river swings northeast, leaving the road and entering the canyon section. Here there is limited access, but also more numerous and larger fish than found the meadow area. Best approach to the canyon section is found near and around the town of Clark, WY.

After leaving the canyon, the river flattens out and flows north into Montana. The lower section is folled by WY 120 and MT 72. Besides cutthroat trout, rainbows, browns and whitefish are available in this lower section. This lower river is wadable and floatable through most of its length.

Goose Lake, Rock Island Lake, Kinsey Lake, Fox Lake and Widewater Lake

These lakes are easily accessed from US 212 near Cooke City, Montana. The popular Goose Lake is located about seven miles north of Cooke City, and contains cutthroat trout up to eighteen inches long. Rock Island Lake contains brookies and cutthroat trout and is found along a trail from the Chief Joseph Campground east of Cooke City. The trail passes Kinsey Lake, which contains some brookies in the sixteen inch range plus cutthroat and lake trout. Neighbors to Rock Island Lake are Fox and Widewater Lakes. Both contain brookies and rainbow trout plus some arctic grayling.

Stillwater River (30)

The Stillwater River heads in the Granite Range of the Beartooth Mts, northeast of Cooke City, Montana, and flows about 50 miles north to join the Yellowstone River at Columbus, Montana. It is reached by driving from the northeast entrance to Red Lodge, then turning west onto MT 78 to Absarokee, Montana, which will place you on the lower reach of the Stillwater. From here you can continue downstream on MT 78, or upstream on MT 420.

Local anglers recognize the Stillwater River as an excellent destination. Fast water and deep pools provide security for rainbows and brown trout in the lower section. The headwater reach offers brookies and cutthroat trout which decline in number after the Mouat Mine section. The lower river has larger fish, probably due to recruitment from the Yellowstone River. The boulder-pocket water holds many fish and shouldn't be ignored. The lower river is a favorite location for bait anglers while the best fly fishing is found in the upper reaches. There are many public fishing access points along the river and most of the fishing is done from the bank.

MESA FALLS ON THE HENRYS FORK

EAST ENTRANCE FISHERIES

Bighorn Lake (31)

Bighorn Lake, a 70 mile long reservoir formed by the Yellowtail Dam in Montana, is located north of Greybull, Wyoming, and south of Billings, Montana. The Bighorn and Shoshone Rivers are the major rivers that create the reservoir, and the entire lake is surrounded by the Bighorn Canyon National Recreation Area.

From the park's east entrance, drive 53 miles to Cody, Wyoming, then take US Alt 14 another 44 miles northeast to Lovell, Wyoming. The National Park Service Visitor Center at Lovell has maps and information to assist in trip planning. From Lovell the southern end of the lake lies twelve miles east via Alt 14. Also from Lovell, WY 37 leads north to Horseshoe Bend, where a marina and boat ramp are located.

The lake is best known as a walleye fishery. Walleye have been caught in the fourteen pound range. Limited rainbow, lake and brown trout, plus many warm water species, are found in the lake. Large mouth bass and channel catfish are the primary fish in the Wyoming portion of the lake. Trolling is the most common approach used for catching the trout.

The lake is usually narrow, with steep sides, and in places is no wider than the rivers that feed the lake. Access is limited for bank anglers, so boating is necessary.

North Fork Shoshone River (32)

US 16 follows this river from the eastern entrance 50 odd miles to Cody, Wyoming. Fishing pressure is heavy, and the river is continually stocked with cutthroat trout. Rainbow, brown, brook trout and whitefish are also frequently caught.

Access is not a problem, and most methods of fishing are used. Downstream from Cody, access to the river is limited and irrigation drawdowns have impacted the fishery. Try this area in the fall for best results. Below Mormon Dam, the river characteristics change and warm water species begin to dominate the fishery.

Wind River (33)

By taking US 120 southeast from Cody, Wyoming, to Thermopolis,Wyoming., the angler will reach the lower Wind River. The 25 mile section of river below Boysen Reservoir to the Bighorn Canal, downstream of Thermopolis, contains rainbow and brown trout, many of which reach trophy size.

Good fishing begins in the spring and lasts through the fall. The canyon section is very popular, and contains big rainbows and brown trout. Wading and bank fishing are the best approaches to effectively fish the pools and pocket water in this section.

After the river leaves the canyon section, floating is the preferred method to reach the fish. Below the "Wedding of the Waters," the Wind River changes its name to the Bighorn River. Below the Bighorn Canal section, warm water species dominate and fewer trout are available.

FISHING DAY HIKES

This sampler of day hikes is recommended for those who want to escape the crowds and experience Yellowstone in its wild glory. Most visitors to Yellowstone (and most visiting anglers) do not hike. Even a two mile stroll will more than repay your efforts.

Before you head out, get a good trail map. The maps in this section are meant to supplement, not replace, a good topographic map. Any time you head into the backcountry, even on a day hike, its a good idea to leave word of your destination with someone.

Spend a little time talking to a park ranger. You'll get excellent advice, an update of trail conditions, and if you're lucky, maybe a fishing tip.

Fires, firearms, and pets are prohibited from the backcountry. Don't ruin a great vacation with a stiff fine. Also, if you pack it in, please pack it out.

For information about extended backcountry visits, see the bibliography at the end of this book. You will need to obtain a backcountry permit only if you are planning to camp overnight. Permits can be obtained up to 48 hrs in advance from any ranger station.

Hellroaring Creek   3 miles

The trailhead is located 3.5 miles from Tower Junction on the Mammoth-Tower Road. The trail descends over 600 feet in the first mile to a suspension bridge over the Yellowstone River. At the two-mile mark there is a junction with the Yellowstone River Trail. When you see the patrol cabin you have reached the creek. A footbridge crosses the creek .5 mile further along the trail.

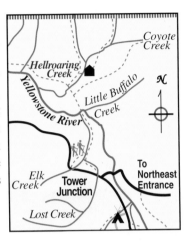

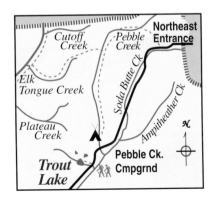

Yellowstone River, Seven Mile Hole   5.1 miles

The trailhead is located at Glacial Boulder, two miles from Canyon Village on the road to Inspiration Point. The trail follows the rim of the Grand Canyon, then descends to the river. The descent is fairly steep and requires strenuous effort on the way out, so be prepared.

Trout Lake   .5 miles

The trailhead is found on the north side of the Northeast Entrance Road about 1.8 miles south of Pebble Creek Campground. The trail climbs over a small ridge then continues to the lake. The hike is short and not very strenuous.

Grizzly Lake 2 miles

The trailhead is located approximately one mile south of Beaver Lake on the Norris-Mammoth Road. The trail cuts through a meadow then climbs a steep hill and enters the forest. The lake is in a narrow valley surrounded by dense timber. The trail descends to the north end of the lake. Take plenty of repellent, for many mosquitoes inhabit this area.

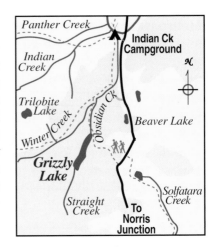

Slough Creek   2 miles

The trailhead is about .5 miles before the Slough Creek Meadows Campground along the Northeast Entrance Road. The trail climbs gradually then descends into the open valley of Slough Creek. You'll find some patrol cabins by the creek and the junction for the Buffalo Plateau Trail. Fishing improves as you go upstream.

McBride Lake 3 miles

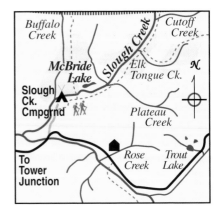

The trailhead is on the east side of the dirt road that leads from the East Entrance Road to Slough Creek Campground, about .5 mile before the camp. Follow the Slough Creek Trail to its junction with the Buffalo Plateau Trail. Cross the creek, following the Buffalo Plateau Trail, then head east across the meadows about one mile to a rocky forested area in which the lake is nestled. The ford across Slough Creek will be difficult if you attempt to cross before mid-July.

Grebe Lake   3 miles

The trailhead is 4 miles west of Canyon Junction on the Norris-Canyon Road. The trail follows an old fire road most of the way. At the two-mile marker, take the trail that forks left. Be prepared to meet many mosquitoes if you go there before the middle of August.

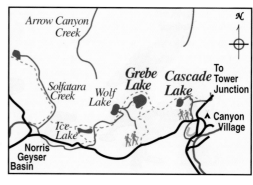

Cascade Lake   2 miles

The trailhead located .5 miles west of Canyon Village on the Norris-Canyon Road. The trail follows Cascade Creek and can be quite muddy until mid-July. Mosquitoes are prevalent, so bring repellent.

Bechler Meadows 3 miles
(Bechler River Bridge 5 miles)

The shortest route begins at Bechler Ranger Station near the end of the Cave Falls Road about 25 miles from Ashton, Idaho. The trail is relatively flat and stays in the forest until you reach Boundary Creek Bridge and enter the meadows. You may be fortunate enough to see whooping cranes in the meadow in July.

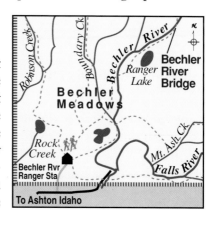

In early summer the meadows are quite swampy and almost impossible to cross, so don't plan to hike there before July. You can follow the river and fish upstream if the meadows are muddy. If not, cross the meadows to the Bechler River Bridge and fish downstream. The mosquitoes and horse flies can be vicious, so take plenty of repellent.

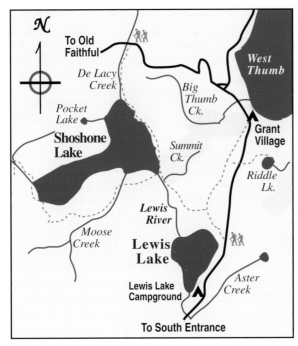

Lewis-Shoshone Channel (Lewis River) 4.5 miles

The trailhead is just north of Lewis Lake about 7 miles south of West Thumb Junction. A fishing trail forks from the main trail and follows the Lewis Lake Shoreline to the channel. The trail is not steep and is easy to follow.

Shoshone Lake (via DeLacy Creek Trail)   3 miles
(Shoshone Lake (via LewisTrail) 4.5 miles)

The DeLacy Creek trailhead is 8 miles east of Old Faithful on the West Thumb Junction Road near Craig Pass. It leads to a shallow portion of the lake and may not be the best choice in mid-summer if you want deep water.

The Lewis trailhead is on South Entrance Road, 7 miles south of West Thumb Junction. Neither trail is steep, and both are easy to follow.

The trailhead is on the South Entrance Road, 5.4 miles south of Grant Village near the north end of Lewis Lake. The first 5 miles of the trail are relatively level and easy to hike. The last 3 miles are mostly downhill to the shore of the lake. In the spring the trail is muddy but tolerable if you're wearing waterproof boots.

Pelican Creek   3 miles

Pelican Valley trailhead is on a spur road north of Squaw Lake, 3 miles east of Fishing Bridge. The trail leads to Pelican Creek Bridge then parallels the creek for 3 miles. The hike is relatively flat.

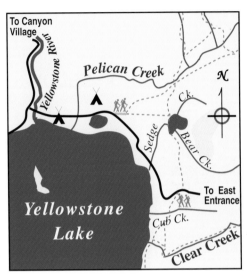

Clear Creek   3 miles

The trailhead is on the East Entrance Road ap-prox-imately 10 miles east of Fishing Bridge. The first 1.5 miles are through forest, then the trail fords Cub Creek. At 2 miles you'll come to the Clear Creek Trail junction. Be sure to take the right fork, which leads to Clear Creek and the Fish and Wildlife fish trapping area. There is a footbridge over Clear Creek down-stream from the trail.

Heart Lake   8 miles

The trailhead is on the South Entrance Road, 5.4 miles south of Grant Village near the north end of Lewis Lake. The first 5 miles of the trail are rela-tively level and easy to hike. The last 3 miles are mostly downhill to the shore of the lake. In the spring the trail is muddy but tolerable if you're wearing waterproof boots.

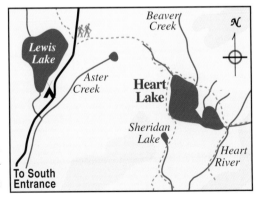

PARK GUIDE DIRECTORY

REGISTERED YELLOWSTONE PARK GUIDES

IDAHO

Allen, Don, Three Rivers Ranch
Box 856, Ashton, ID 83420
208/652-3750

Lawson, Mike   Henry's Fork Anglers
Box 487, St. Anthony, ID 83445
208/558-7525

Schnebly, Scott   Lost River Outfitters
P.O. Box 3445, Ketchum, ID 83340
208/726-1706

Sessions, Lynn   Last Chance Lodge and
Outfitters
HC 66, Box 482, Island Park, ID 83429
208/558-7068

MONTANA

Anderson, George   Yellowstone Angler
Highway 89 S.   Livingston, MT 59047
406/222-7130

Bannon, Patrick   Montana Flyfishing
Adventures
P.O. Box 64, Deer Lodge, MT 59722
406/846-0002

Bethel, Howard   Hawkridge Outfitters
8000 Trail Ck Rd. Livingston, MT 59715
406/585-9608

Bingman, J.D.   Wild Trout Outfitters
Box 3, Big Sky, MT 59716
406/995-4895

Blount, Gary David
Yellowstone Catch & Release Outfitter
P.O. Box 741 West Yellowstone, MT 59758
406/646-9082

Bretz, Paul   Bretz Professional Fly Fishing
301 South 7th St.
Livingston, MT 59047
406/222-7375

Combs, Tim   The Tackle Shop
P.O. Box 624, Ennis, MT 59729
406/682-4263

Criner, Jim   The Trout Shop
Box 698, West Yellowstone, MT 59758
406/646-7801

Corcoran, David   The River's Edge
2012 North 7th Ave. Bozeman, MT 59715
406/586-5373

Cunningham, Robert
P.O. Box 311 Gallatin Gateway, MT 59730
406/763-4761

Evans, Gary   Madison Valley Cabins
P.O. Box 525 Cameron, MT 59720
406/763-4890

French, Steve   Gallatin River Guides
Box 212, Big Sky, MT 59716
406/995-4369

Howard, Stuart Running River Fly Guide
113 West Villard Bozeman, MT 59715
406/586-1788

Howe, Katherine Sun Raven Guide Service
Route 38, Box 2163, Livingston, MT 59047
406/333-4454

Hull, Dan Madison River Outfitters
Box 398, West Yellowstone, MT 59758
406/646-9644

Jacklin, Robert Jacklin's Inc.
Box 310, West Yellowstone, MT 59758
406/646-7336

Keenan, John Tim Miner Lodge
Rt. 1 Box 660, Emigrant, MT 59027
406/848-7525

Kircher, John Boyne U.S.A.
P.O. Box 1, Big Sky, MT 59716
406/995-4211

Klassen, Stan Firehole Ranch
P.O. Box 11500, Hebgen Lake
West Yellowstone, MT 59758
406/646-7294

Lund, Kurt Lund Outfitters
P.O. Box 686, West Yellowstone, MT 59758
406/646-7294

Matthews, Craig Blue Ribbon Flies
Box 1037, West Yellowstone, MT 59758
406/646-9365

Miller, Larry Sleepy Hollow Lodge
Box 1080, West Yellowstone, MT 59758
406/646-7707

Moore, H. A. Rendezvous Outfitters
P.O. Box 447, Gardiner, MT 59030
406/848-7967

Muller, Bruce Voss Inn
319 S. Wilson, Bozeman, MT 59715
406/587-0892

Parks, Richard Park's Fly Shop
Box 196, Gardiner, MT 59030
406/848-7314

Parsch, Brad East Slope Anglers
Box 261, Big Sky, MT 59716
406/995-4369

Rice, Paul
Route 85, Box 4194 Livingston, MT 59047
406/222-1522

Reiner, Dean Hatch Finders
120 South M St. Livingston, MT 59047
406/222-0989

Rizzotto, Carman High Country Outfitters
Route 1, Box 515, Pray, MT 59065
406/333-4763

Scherer, Lee Still Waters Outfitting
3234 Reimers Park, Billings, MT 59102
406/652-8111

Siegle, Dale Blue Ribbon Fishing Tours
209 Blue Heron Dr. Livingston, MT 59047
406/222-7714

Smith, Jennifer High Country Angler Inc.
Box 132, Bozeman, MT 59771
406/587-5140

Swanson, Arrick Arrick's Fishing Flies
128 Madison, West Yellowstone, MT 59758
406/646-7290

Travis, Tom Montana's Master Angler
Box 1320, Livingston, MT 59047
406/222-2273

Watson, Lee Lee Watson Outfitter
P.O. Box 7104, Bozeman, MT 59771
406/586-3181

Williams, Don Williams Guide Service
P.O. Box 2, Livingston, MT 59047
406/222-1386

WYOMING

Aune, Scott Aune's Absaroka Angler
1390 Sheridan Ave. Cody, WY 82414
307/587-5105

Bressler, Joe Vern Bressler Outfitters, Inc.
Box 766, Wilson, WY 83014
307/733-6934

Cole, Pat Yellowstone Association
P.O. Box 117, Yellowstone Park, WY
82190
307/344-2293

Coy, Thomas Coy's Wilderness Float
Trips
Box 3356, Jackson, WY 83001
307/733-6726

Hocking, Scott Teton Troutfitters
Box 536, Wilson, WY 83014
307/733-5362

Ingold, Edward Rivermeadows Inc.
Box 347, Wilson, WY 83014
307/733-9263

James, Bruce Jack Dennis Outdoor Shop
Box 286, Jackson, WY 83001
307/733-3270

Jones, Dean Reel Adventures
3455 S. Tensleep #19, Jackson, WY 83001
307/733-4651

Landis, Dean Rocky Mtn Ministries
Star Route Box 373, Jackson, WY 83001
307/733-6540

Lee, John John Lee Outfitting
P.O. Box 8368, Jackson, WY 83001
307/733-9441

Meeks, Noel Hidden Basin Outfitters,
Inc.
Box 7182, Jackson, WY 83001

307/733-7980
Moore, Scott Camp Creek Inn
Star Route, Box 45-B, Jackson, WY 83001
307/733-3099

Perkins, Donald Snake River Kayak
& Canoe School
P.O. Box 3482, Jackson, WY 83001
307/733-3127

Pomeroy, R. Westbank Anglers
Box 523, Teton Village, WY 83025
307/733-6483

Richards, Bob Mr. Grub Steak
Expeditions
P.O. Box 1013, Cody, WY 82414
307/527-6316

Wilson, Bryon Grassy Lake Outfitters
P.O. Box 853, Jackson, WY 83001
307/733-6779

OTHER

Appleton, David Outpost Wilderness
Box 7, Lake George, CO 80827

Goetz, Joe Wilderness Inquiry
1313 5th St. SE Suite 117
Minneapolis, MN 55414
612/379-3858

Mentzer, Gregory Montana River Guides
3 Edgebrook Way, Newark, DE 19702
302/738-3497

Miller, Mary Educo School of Colorado
5569 North County Rd #29
Loveland, CO 80538
303/679-4339

Olsen, Robert & Chad Greater
Yellowstone Flyfishers
1269 S. Drexel Way, Lakewood, CO 80232
303/985-3537

INDEX
OF WATERS

ABOUT THE AUTHOR

Robert Charlton's love of the Yellowstone country began when he worked as a camp counselor at Lake-of-the-Woods, near the park boundary. He has since fished the Yellowstone back country extensively, and been the source of many a "you should have been there yesterday" rumor in the Yellowstone area. His home on the banks of the Henry's Fork of the Snake River in St. Anthony, Idaho is well positioned for his frequent outings in the park.

Born in Utah, he received a Ph.D. in Professional Psychology from Utah State University. He subsequently moved to Idaho, where he lives with his wife, Linda, and their four children.